H. J. DRAPER.

SCENE IN HALL OF A HIGHLAND CHIEFTAIN IN THE SEVENTEENTH CENTURY.

A BARD RECITING THE DEEDS OF THE CLAN.

SERGT. JAMES SUTHERLAND,   ADAM SUTHERLAND,   NEIL MACKAY.
3rd Suthd. R.V., Dall, Brora,   *Gordon Bush, Strath Brora,*   *Hope Durness,*
Sutherlandshire.   *Sutherlandshire.*   *Sutherlandshire.*

SCOTTISH HIGHLANDERS ON THE EVE OF THE GREAT MIGRATION 1725–1775

THE NORTHERN HIGHLANDS

by
David Dobson

CLEARFIELD

Copyright © 2007 by David Dobson
All Rights Reserved.

Printed for
Clearfield Company by
Genealogical Publishing Co.
Baltimore, Maryland
2007

ISBN-13: 978-0-8063-5363-0
ISBN-10: 0-8063-5363-5

Made in the United States of America

INTRODUCTION

Emigration from Scotland to colonial America, which had been small scale during the seventeenth century, became significant during the eighteenth century. Much of this exodus originated in the Highlands of Scotland where the traditional social and economic structures were beginning to break down under pressure from the Commercial and the Industrial Revolutions which were occurring in both England and Lowland Scotland. Profits were to be made by supplying raw materials and foodstuffs to the growing factory towns. Clan chiefs increasingly abandoned their patriarchal role in favour of becoming capitalist landlords, and the traditional social fabric of the Highlands was soon in tatters. This social breakdown was also intensified through the failure of the Jacobite cause in 1746 followed by the military occupation and repression that occurred in the Highlands in the aftermath of Culloden. The absorption of the great Highland landowners and clan chiefs into the British elite ultimately resulted in farm rents being increased to enable the landowners to maintain their new lifestyles. Voluntary emigration by Gaelic-speaking Highlanders began in the 1730s when groups left Argyll bound for North Carolina and New York, and others from Inverness bound for Georgia. In 1746 the British Government despatched about one thousand Jacobites, prisoners of war, in chains as indentured servants bound for the colonies. During the Seven Years War, 1756 to 1763, Highland Regiments were raised for the first time. In North America, this military struggle between Britain and France was known as the French and Indian War, in which regiments such as Fraser's Highlanders and Montgomery's Highlanders played a significant role. Many of the soldiers chose to settle in the former French Canada and in America rather than return to Scotland. These military settlers, and their families and friends who followed, formed a substantial portion of the Highlanders who settled in the years before the outbreak of the American Revolution in 1776. The 1760s and early 1770s were the peak periods for Highland emigration in the eighteenth century. After 1783 the emphasis of Highland settlement was in Canada although emigration to America continued to a lesser degree. Highland emigration was also a result of a significant population increase in an area with limited resources.

What resources are available to those wishing to trace their immigrant ancestors of the eighteenth century from the Highlands of Scotland? The most important sources of information are the Old Parish Registers of the Church of Scotland, which provide data on baptisms and marriages. While this is generally successful for eighteenth-century research covering Lowland Scotland, there are severe limitations on their use for Highland research. In the absence of church records, family historians have to turn to a miscellany of other records, such as court records, estate papers, sasines, gravestone inscriptions, burgess rolls, port books, services of heirs, wills and testaments, rent rolls, and in this case, particularly, militia records. The latter two sources establish where and when particular families were settled and so provide sites to which genealogists can link.

This series is designed to identify the kind of material that is important in the absence of church records and will supplement the church registers when they are available. This volume deals with the Northern Highlands, an area which includes the counties of Caithness, Sutherland, Ross and Cromarty, a location from which many of the pioneer emigrants who settled in colonial Georgia, North Carolina, Pennsylvania, New York, and the Canadian Maritimes originated. Among the vessels which transported emigrants from the north of Scotland to such areas were the Hector to Nova Scotia in 1773, the Friendship to Philadelphia in 1774, and the Peace and Plenty to New York in 1774. This book does not claim to be a comprehensive directory of all the people of the Northern Highlands during the mid-eighteenth century but rather is an attempt to demonstrate the range and quality of material available. One of the most useful sources has been the militia lists which identified some of the Highlanders who opposed the Jacobites in 1745-1746. The main clans which were traditionally associated with the Northern Highlands were the Mackays, the McLeods, the Sutherlands, the Sinclairs, the Gunns, the Munros, the Rosses, and the Mackenzies, all of whom are well represented in this volume.

David Dobson
St Andrews, Scotland, 2007

Badgall Bay, Edrachillis; on the Western Coast.

SOURCES

F	=	Fastii Ecclesiae Scoticanae, J. Scott. [Edinburgh, 1915]
MCP	=	More Culloden Papers, 1626-1747, D. Warrand, [Inverness, 1930]
NAS	=	National Archives of Scotland
OR	=	Old Ross-shire and Scotland [Tain and Balnagown Documents], W. MacGill, London, 1909.
SA	=	John Home's Survey of Assynt, [Edinburgh, 1960]
SCA	=	Scottish Catholic Archives, Edinburgh
TGSI	=	Transactions of the Gaelic Society of Inverness, series

SCOTTISH HIGHLANDERS ON THE EVE OF THE GREAT MIGRATION 1725-1775: THE PEOPLE OF THE NORTHERN HIGHLANDS

ABRACH, NEIL, in Unapool, Assynt, Sutherland, Sutherland, 1774. [SA#88]

ADAM, JOHN, a writer in Thurso, Caithness, 1758. [NAS.GD84/2/44]

ADAMSON, HUGH, a tenant farmer in Cruick, Halladale, Caithness, 1756. [NAS.GD87.SEC2.13]

ALLAN, DONALD, a cottar in Gills, Mey, Caithness, 1771. [NAS.GD96.679.14]

ALLAN, JOHN, mariner, born 1719, died 1772, father of Neil and John both shipmasters in Greenock. [Lochcarron, Wester Ross, gravestone]

ANDERSON, GEORGE, a merchant in Cromarty, c1766. [NAS.RS38.XII.274]

ANDERSON, JAMES, a bailie of Fortrose, the Black Isle, 1734. [NAS.RS38.IX.135]

ANDERSON, JOHN, merchant burgess of Wick, Caithness, 1746. [NAS.B73.2/1/9-10]

ANGUS, ELIZABETH, a cottar in Mey, Caithness, 1771. [NAS.GD96.679.14]

AULD, JAMES, tenant farmer in Eastside of Mey, Caithness, 1771. [NAS.GD96.679.14]

AULD, WILLIAM, a cottar in Mey, Caithness. 1771. [NAS.GD96.679.14]

BACKIE, JOHN, a cottar in Mey, Caithness, 1771.
[NAS.GD96.679.14]

BACKIE, KENNETH, a cottar in Mey, Caithness, 1771.
[NAS.GD96.679.14]

BAILLIE, ALEXANDER, Dean of Guild of Tain, Easter Ross, 1766. [OR#408]

BAILLIE, JOHN, factor in Cromarty, the Black Isle, 1749.
[NAS.E746.16]

BAILLIE, WILLIAM, of Rosehall, 1766. [OR#408]

BAIN, ALEXANDER, in Unapool, Assynt, Sutherland, 1774.
[SA#88]

BAIN, DONALD, in Unapool, Assynt, Sutherland, 1774.
[SA#88]

BAIN, DUNCAN, in Lagginteamore, Applecross, Wester Ross, 1718. [TGSI.LIV.450]

BAIN, GEORGE, a cottar in Mey, Caithness, 1771.
[NAS.GD96.679.14]

BAIN, HUGH, a tenant farmer in Dalalvah, Halladale, Caithness, 1756. [NAS.GD87.SEC2.13]

BAIN, JAMES, a cottar in Mey, Caithness, 1771.
[NAS.GD96.679.14]

BAIN, JOHN, in Auchnadroil, Applecross, Wester Ross, 1718.
[TGSI.LIV.451]

BAIN, JOHN, in Golvell, soldier of Captain Hugh McKay's Independent Company, 17 June 1746. [TGSI.LIII.390]

BAIN, JOHN, in Knocknach, Assynt, Sutherland, 1774.
[SA#76]

BAIN, RORY, in Duchlash, Assynt, Sutherland, 1774. [SA#79]

BAIN, WILLIAM, in Sandego, soldier of Captain Hugh McKay's Independent Company, 17 June 1746. [TGSI.LIII.390]

BAIN, Mrs, widow of Kenneth Bain, in Unapool, Assynt, Sutherland, 1774. [SA#88]

BAKIE, JAMES, and son, tenants in Harrow, Mey, Caithness, 1771. [NAS.GD96.679.14]

BALFOUR, GEORGE, born 1724, son of John Dalfour minister in Nigg, Easter Ross, educated at Marischal College, Aberdeen, apprenticed to a merchant in Edinburgh, minister of Tain, , Easter Ross, from 1750 to 1798, died 18 October 1798. Husband of Barbara Rose, and parents of Chalmers, Isobel, John, Jean, and Katherine. [F.7.75]

BALFOUR, JOHN, minister of Nigg, Easter Ross, from 1729 to 1752, died 6 February 1752. Husband of Isabella Dow, and parents of George, Christian, Jean, Elizabeth, and John. [F.7.66]

BANE, JOHN, with his wife and three children, in Oldany, Assynt, Sutherland, 1774. [SA#85]

BANKS, ANDREW, a cottar in Mey, Caithness, 1771. [NAS.GD96.679.14]

BANKS, DONALD, cottar in Eastside of Mey, Caithness, 1771. [NAS.GD96.679.14]

BANKS, DONALD, tenant in Mill of Mey, Caithness, 1771. [NAS.GD96.679.14]

BANKS, JAMES, testament, 1735. [NAS.GD96.683.1]

BANKS, JAMES, tenant in Eastside of Mey, Caithness, 1771. [NAS.GD96.679.14]

BANKS, JOHN, a cottar in Mey, Caithness, 1771. [NAS.GD96.679.14]

BANKS, MAGNUS, tenant in Eastside of Mey, Caithness, 1771. [NAS.GD96.679.14]

BANKS, WILLIAM, tenant in Eastside of Mey, Caithness, 1771. [NAS.GD96.679.14]

BARCLAY, ROBERT, in Clayside, soldier of Alexander Gunn's Independent Company at Shiromore, 16 June 1746. [TGSI.LIII.368]

BARNETSON, JOHN, a cottar and tenant in Mill of Mey, Caithness, 1771. [NAS.GD96.679.14]

BARNETSON, THOMAS, a cottar in Mey, Caithness, 1771. [NAS.GD96.679.14]

BAXTER, WILLIAM, a soldier in Captain Hugh McLeod of Geanies Independent Company on 17 June 1746. [TGSI.LIII.381]

BAYNE, JOHN, born 1690 son of John Bayne in Dingwall, Ross and Cromarty, educated at Edinburgh University, minister of Dingwall, from 1716 to 1737, died 3 February 1737. Husband of Ann Bethune, parents of Ann, Christian, and Jean. [F.7.34]

BEAN, DONALD, in Belnain, soldier of Captain Colin Mackenzie's Independent Company, 1746. [TGSI.LIII.385]

BEATON, ALEXANDER, soldier of Captain George Mackay's Independent Company at Shiromore, 1746. [TGSI.LIII.370]

BEATON, DUNCAN, in Cranack, soldier of Captain Colin Mackenzie's Independent Company, 1746. [TGSI.LIII.385]

BEATON, FARQUHAR, in Cainloch, soldier of Captain Colin Mackenzie's Independent Company, 1746. [TGSI.LIII.385]

BEATON, FINLAY, in Belnain, soldier of Captain Colin Mackenzie's Independent Company, 1746. [TGSI.LIII.385]

BEATON, JOHN, tacksman of Dingwall, Ross and Cromarty, 1767-1773. [NAS.GD46.SEC.1/212]

BEATON, MURDO, tacksman of Dingwall, Ross and Cromarty, 1767. [NAS.GD46.SEC.1/212]

BEGG, ALEXANDER, miller, tenant in Gills, Mey, Caithness, 1771. [NAS.GD96.679.14]

BELL, DONALD, in Dornoch, soldier of Alexander Gunn's Independent Company at Shiromore, 16 June 1746. [TGSI.LIII.368]

BENDERMAN, WILLIAM, soldier of Alexander Gunn's Independent Company at Shiromore, 16 June 1746. [TGSI.LIII.368]

BETHUNE, ANGUS, a miller, with his wife, two children, and one servant in Culaig, Assynt, Sutherland, 1774. [SA#77]

BETHUNE, DANIEL, born 1679, eldest son of Kenneth Bethune of Skeabost, educated at Marischal College, Aberdeen, minister of Ardesier from 1713 to 1717, minister of Rosskeen from 1717 to 1754, died 15 March 1754. Husband of (1) Grizell Russell, parents of Isobel, Anne, Janet, Margaret, James, Peter, James, William, Elizabeth, and Kenneth; (2) Katherine Wilson. [F.7.68]

BETHUNE, JOHN, born 1725 son of Reverend Farquhar Bethune in Croy, educated at Marischal College, Aberdeen, St Andrews, and Edinburgh, a tutor, minister of Rosskeen from 1754 to 1774, died 15 April 1774. Husband of Janet Bethune, parents of Grizell, Margaret, and Mary. [F.7.68]

BEYN, or ROY, RORIE, soldier of Captain Alexander Mackenzie's Independent Company, dead by 1746. [TGSI.LIII.382]

BIZET, LEWIS, in Tain, Easter Ross, 1766. [OR#409]

BOWER, JOHN, a cottar in Mey, Caithness, 1771. [NAS.GD96.679.14]

BOWIE, RODERICK, a tenant in Forsinard, Halladale, Caithness, 1756. [NAS.GD87.SEC2.13]

BROCH, WILLIAM, tenant in Eastside of Mey, Caithness, 1771. [NAS.GD96.679.14]

BRODIE, ALEXANDER, minister of Reay, Caithness, from 1723 to 1729, died 1729. Father of Alexander. [F.7.132]

BRODIE, CHARLES, a merchant in Ardnasier, 1758. [NAS.GD87.Sec.2/17]

BRODIE, GEORGE, minister of Durness, Sutherland, in 1715, then minister of Eddrachillis, Sutherland, from 1724 to 1740, died 1 March 1740. Husband of Barbara Mackay, and father of William, Henrietta, Margaret, and Christian. [F.7.104]

BRODIE, JAMES, born 1708 in Caithness. Minister of Canisbay, Caithness, from 1747 to 1779, died 5 December 1779. Husband of Isabella Corse, and father of William and Henrietta. [F.7.117]

BRODIE, JAMES, born 1707, son of Reverend Alexander Brodie in Reay, Caithness. Minister of Latheron, Caithness, from 1734 to 1774, died 6 November 1774. Husband of Anne Murray and father of Samuel, James, Margaret, Patrick, Alexander, George, and Richard. [F.7.126]

BRUCE, DONALD, a cottar in Mey, Caithness, 1771. [NAS.GD96.679.14]

BRUCE, JAMES, a cottar in Mey, Caithness, 1771.
[NAS.GD96.679.14]

BRUCE, JOHN, a cottar in Gills, Mey, Caithness, 1771.
[NAS.GD96.679.14]

BRUCE, SAMUEL. a cottar in Gills, Mey, Caithness, 1771.
[NAS.GD96.679.14]

BUIE, WILLIAM, in Buy, soldier of Captain Hugh McKay's Independent Company, 17 June 1746. [TGSI.LIII.391]

BUY, ALEXANDER, a weaver in Tain, Easter Ross, 1766. [OR#409]

BUY, or MCKENZIE, FARQUHAR, with his wife, in Unapool, Assynt, Sutherland, 1774. [SA#88]

BUY, THOMAS, in Cruick, a soldier of the Master of Ross' Independent Company at Linachan, 14 June 1746. [TGSI.LIII.392]

CALDELL, JOHN, in Spingidell, Sutherland, soldier of Alexander Gunn's Independent Company at Shiromore, 16 June 1746. [TGSI.LIII.368]

CALDER, PATRICK, of Lynager, parish of Watten, Caithness, 1762. [NAS.GD139.228]

CALDER, WILLIAM, town clerk of Wick, Caithness, eldest son of John Calder baillie of Wick, 1745. [NAS.GD139.40], messenger and notary in Wick, son of the late John Calder, merchant there, 24 March 1756. [NAS.GD136.73]

CALLUM, WILLIAM, in Knockbean, soldier of Captain Colin Mackenzie's Independent Company, 1746. [TGSI.LIII.384]

CAMERON, EVAN, in Kiltearn, soldier of George Munro of Culcairns' Independent Company, 1745. [TGSI.LIII.364]

CAMERON, JAMES, in Katwall, soldier of George Munro of Culcairns' Independent Company, 1745. [TGSI.LIII.364]

CAMERON, JOHN, born 1734 in Ferintosh. Schoolmaster at Tain, , Easter Ross, from 1766 to 1768, minister of Halkirk, Caithness, from 1769 to 1821, died 9 December 1821. Husband of Mary Lee, and father of Sarah. [F.7.122]

CAMERON, JOHN, tenant in Dalkinloch, 1770. [NAS.E746.167.5]

CAMPBELL, Ensign ALEXANDER, tenant farmer, with his wife, two children, and three servants, in Inver, Assynt, Sutherland, 1774. [SA#67/81]

CAMPBELL, ANGUS, with his wife, in Torbreck, Assynt, Sutherland, 1774. [SA#87]

CAMPBELL, CHRISTIAN, with her son, in Culaig, Assynt, Sutherland, 1774. [SA#77]

CAMPBELL, DONALD, with his wife, four children, two servants, and his father, in Ardvar, Assynt, Sutherland, 1774. [SA#72]

CAMPBELL, GEORGE, in Knockdow, soldier of Captain Hugh McKay's Independent Company, 17 June 1746. [TGSI.LIII.390]

CAMPBELL, HUGH, educated at Marischal College, Aberdeen, ordained 1707, minister of Knockbain, Ross and Cromarty, 1721 to 1746, died 18 July 1746. Husband of Henrietta, daughter of Colin Campbell of Delnies and Mary Duff, parents of Mary, William, Colin, Catherine, Archibald, John, Hugh, and Anne. [F.7.15]

CAMPBELL, JOHN, sergeant of Alexander Gunn's Independent Company at Shiromore, 16 June 1746. [TGSI.LIII.369]

CAMPBELL, JOHN, a cooper in Tain, Easter Ross, 1766. [OR#408]

CAMPBELL, NEIL, with his wife, four children, and two servants, in Ardvar, Assynt, Sutherland, 1774. [SA#73]

CAMPBELL, ROBERT, in Islandhoan, soldier of Captain Hugh McKay's Independent Company, 17 June 1746. [TGSI.LIII.390]

CAMPBELL, RODERICK, in Alness, Easter Ross, soldier of George Munro of Culcairns' Independent Company, 1745. [TGSI.LIII.364]

CAMPBELL, WILLIAM, in Cowie, soldier of George Munro of Culcairns' Independent Company, 1745. [TGSI.LIII.364]

CAMPBELL, WILLIAM, in Ederton, a soldier of the Master of Ross' Independent Company at Linachan, 14 June 1746. [TGSI.LIII.392]

CAMPBELL, WILLIAM, farmer in Achowramscraig, died 1753, his wife Barbara Gunn died in March 1766. [Kirkton gravestone, Melvich, Sutherland]

CHISHOLM, DAVID, born 1723 son of Rev. Thomas Chisholm, educated at King's College, Aberdeen, minister of Kilmorack from 1754 to 1768, died 13 April 1768. Husband of Jean Inglis, parents of Robert, John, Alexander, Jean Wardlaw, and Christain. [F.7.39]

CHISHOLM, FINLAY, in Attadaile, soldier of Captain Alexander Mackenzie's Independent Company, 1746. [TGSI.LIII.383]

CHISHOLM, MALCOLM, soldier of Captain Alexander Mackenzie's Independent Company, 1746. [TGSI.LIII.383]

CHISHOLM, THOMAS, born 1680, son of Alexander Chisholm of Teawig, minister of Kilmorack from 1711 to 1754, died 6 January 1768. Father of Robert (died abroad 1745), James, David, John, Thomas, Primrose, and Katherine. [F.7.39]

CHISHOLM, WILLIAM, in Drumnaick, a soldier of the Master of Ross' Independent Company at Linachan, 14 June 1746. [TGSI.LIII.392]

CLARK, DONALD, in Kildinn, soldier of Captain Colin Mackenzie's Independent Company, 1746. [TGSI.LIII.385]

CLARK, DONALD, tacksman of Dingwall, Ross and Cromarty, 1767-1773. [NAS.GD46.SEC.1/212]

CLARK, DONALD, a cottar in Mey, Caithness, 1771. [NAS.GD96.679.14]

CLARK, GEORGE, tacksman of Dingwall, Ross and Cromarty, 1767-1773. [NAS.GD46.SEC.1/212]

CLARK, JAMES, a shoemaker in Tain, Easter Ross, 1766. [OR#409]

CLARK, JOHN, soldier of Captain George Mackay's Independent Company at Shiromore, 1746. [TGSI.LIII.370]

CLARK, WILLIAM, tacksman of Dingwall, Ross and Cromarty, 1767. [NAS.GD46.SEC.1/212]

CLARKE, JAMES, of Clashneach, born 1705, died 30 March 1774, his wife Margaret Mackay, born 1726, died 29 September 1805. [Balnakeil gravestone, Sutherland]

CLERK, ALEXANDER, the younger, a soldier in Captain Hugh McLeod of Geanies Independent Company on 17 June 1746. [TGSI.LIII.380]

CLYNE, HELEN, a cottar in Mey, Caithness, 1771. [NAS.GD96.679.14]

CLYNE, JOHN, a cottar in Mey, Caithness, 1771. [NAS.GD96.679.14]

CONNELL, JAMES, a fox-hunter in the barony of Coigach, 1773. [NAS.E746.147]

COOK, JOHN, a weaver in Tain, Easter Ross, 1766. [OR#409]

CORSE, HUGH, born 1676, minister of Bower, Caithness, from 1701 to 1738, died 6 July 1738. Husband of Janet Munro, and father of John and Isabella. [F.7.114]

CRAMOND, WILLIAM, a wright in Tain, Easter Ross, 1766. [OR#408]

CREACH, DAVID, in Brabster, Caithness, 1765. [NAS.GD139.229]

CROMARTY, JAMES, tenant in Eastside of Mey, Caithness, 1771. [NAS.GD96.679.14]

CRUVACH, JOHN, a tenant in Halladale, Caithness, 1756. [NAS.GD87.SEC2.13]

CUMMING, JAMES, of Sluy, 1756. [NAS.GD139.41/3]

DAVIDSON, DONALD, soldier of Captain Alexander Mackenzie's Independent Company, dead by 1746. [TGSI.LIII.383]

DAVIDSON, DONALD, a wright in Tain, Easter Ross, 1766. [OR#408]

DAVIDSON, JOHN, tacksman of Rosemarkie, the Black Isle, 1774. [NAS.GD46.SEC.1/212]

DAVIE, DONALD, in Obsdeall, soldier of George Munro of Culcairns' Independent Company, 1745. [TGSI.LIII.364]

DAWSON, POLSON, in Tain, Easter Ross, 1766. [OR#409]

DENOON, ANDREW, in Tain, Easter Ross, 1766. [OR#409]

DENOON, DAVID, born 1723 in Inverness, educated at King's College, Aberdeen, ordained 1758. Minister of

Killearnan, Ross and Cromarty, from 1758 to 1790, died 2 January 1792. Husband of (1) Mary Inglis, parents of Hugh, Catherine, David, and Jean; (2) Janet Beton. [F.7.12]

DENOON, RONALD, in Tain, Easter Ross, 1766. [OR#409]

DINGWALL, RANALD, at Ballachragan, 1780. [NAS.E746.81]

DONACHY, CHRISTIAN NEIN, in Achachork, Applecross, Wester Ross, 1718. [TGSI.LIV.452]

DOUGLAS, CHRISTIAN, with one servant, in Stronchrubie, Assynt, Sutherland, 1774. [SA#87]

DOUGLAS, DUNCAN, corporal of George Munro of Culcairns' Independent Company, 1745. [TGSI.LIII.364]

DOULL, PATRICK, a merchant in Thurso, Caithness, 1758. [NAS.GD84/2/45; GD87.Sec.2/15]

DOULL, PETER, son in law of Katherine, Dowager Lady Bighouse, 1747. [NAS.GD87.Sec.2/12]

DOUN, or MCLEOD, ALEXANDER, with his wife, two children, and one servant in Culaig, Assynt, Sutherland, 1774. [SA#77]

DOW, DONALD, soldier of Captain Alexander Mackenzie's Independent Company, 1746. [TGSI.LIII.383]

DOW, DUNCAN, in Attadaile, soldier of Captain Alexander Mackenzie's Independent Company, 1746. [TGSI.LIII.382]

DOWN, DONALD, in Glachour, soldier of Captain Colin Mackenzie's Independent Company, 1746. [TGSI.LIII.384]

DOWN, GILBERT, soldier of Captain Hugh McKay's Independent Company, 17 June 1746. [TGSI.LIII.390]

DUFF, HUGH, minister of Fearn, Ross and Cromarty, from 1698 to 1739, died 3 July 1739. Father of William and Hugh. [F.7.56]

DUNBAR, DAVID, born 1716, son of John Dunbar of Kincorth. Minister of Olrig, Caithness, from 1735 to 1761, died 13 July 1761. Husband of Mary Dunbar, and father of Mary, Marjory, and John. [F.7.129]

DUNBAR, ISOBEL, wife of John Ross a vinetuner at Dunrobin, Sutherland, died on 18 March 1727. [Golspie gravestone, Sutherland]

DUNBAR, JAMES, sailor or fisherman settled at New Tarbat, Easter Ross, 1765. [NAS.E746.80]

DUNCAN, ALEXANDER, tacksman of Lochalsh and Letterfern, Wester Ross, 1766. [NAS.GD46.SEC.1/212]

DUNCAN, JAMES, a cottar in Mey, Caithness, 1771. [NAS.GD96.679.14]

DUNDAS, ALEXANDER, a cottar in Mey, Caithness, 1771. [NAS.GD96.679.14]

DUNNET, DAVID, tenant in Gills, Mey, Caithness, 1771. [NAS.GD96.679.14]

DUNNET, GEORGE, tenant in Eastside of Mey, Caithness, 1771. [NAS.GD96.679.14]

DUNNET, GEORGE, tenant in Quoy, Eastside of Mey, Caithness, 1771. [NAS.GD96.679.14]

DUNNET, JAMES, a cottar in Mey, Caithness, 1771. [NAS.GD96.679.14]

DUNNET, JOHN, a merchant in Thurso, Caithness, 1730s. [NAS.SC14.78.30; AC8.552]

DUNNET, JOHN, tenant in Mey, Caithness, 1771. [NAS.GD96.679.14]

DUNNET, JOHN tenant in Eastside of Mey, Caithness, 1771.
[NAS.GD96.679.14]

DUNNET, KATHERINE, a cottar in Mey, Caithness, 1771.
[NAS.GD96.679.14]

DUNNET, MALCOLM, a cottar in Gills, Mey, Caithness,
1771. [NAS.GD96.679.14]

DUNNET, THEODORE, in Thurso, Caithness, 1735.
[NAS.GD96.700]

DUNNET, THOMAS, a cottar in Mey, Caithness, 1771.
[NAS.GD96.679.14]

DUNSTAN, THOMAS, tenant in Eastside of Mey, Caithness,
1771. [NAS.GD96.679.14]

EDIE, DONALD, master of the Betty of Dunrobin, 1743;
master of the Betty of Cromarty, 1745. [NAS.E504.17.1]

EDIE, WILLIAM, soldier of Captain Hugh McKay's
Independent Company, 17 June 1746. [TGSI.LIII.390]

FALCONER, ALEXANDER, born 1730 in Inverness,
graduated from King's College, Aberdeen, in 1750,
minister of Eddrachillis, Sutherland, from 1763 to 1802,
died 14 May 1802. Husband of Mary McIntosh, and
father of Helen, Fairly, Barbara, Joanna, Mary, Anne,
John, James, Alexander, James, George and Lachlan.
[F.7.105]

FEARN, DAVID, in Cambuscurry, a soldier of the Master of
Ross' Independent Company at Linachan, 14 June 1746.
[TGSI.LIII.391]

FERGUSON, CHRISTOPHER, tacksman of Urray, Ross and
Cromarty, 1767-1773. [NAS.GD46.SEC.1/212]

FERGUSON, JOHN, in Ardoch, soldier of George Munro of
Culcairns' Independent Company, 1745. [TGSI.LIII.364]

FERGUSON, WILLIAM, in Brahan, soldier of Captain Colin Mackenzie's Independent Company, 1746. [TGSI.LIII.385]

FERME, JAMES, minister of Wick, Caithness, from 1727 to 1760, died 9 October 1760. Husband of (1) Elizabeth Munro, and (2) Margaret Dunbar. [F.7.142]

FINLAY, ROBERT, educated at Edinburgh University, minister of Rosemarkie, the Black Isle, from 1708 to 1733, died 4 December 1733. Husband of Katherine Denoon. [F.7.23]

FINLAYSON, ARCHIBALD, soldier of Captain Alexander Mackenzie's Independent Company, dead by 1746. [TGSI.LIII.382]

FINLAYSON, DONALD, in Rerraig, soldier of Captain Alexander Mackenzie's Independent Company, 1746. [TGSI.LIII.383]

FINLAYSON, DONALD, in Achonilech, soldier of Captain Alexander Mackenzie's Independent Company, dead by 1746. [TGSI.LIII.383]

FINLAYSON, DUNCAN, soldier of Captain Alexander Mackenzie's Independent Company, dead by 1746. [TGSI.LIII.382]

FINLAYSON, DUNCAN, in Lochalsh, soldier of Captain Alexander Mackenzie's Independent Company, dead by 1746. [TGSI.LIII.382]

FINLAYSON, KENNETH ROY, soldier of Captain Alexander Mackenzie's Independent Company, 1746. [TGSI.LIII.382]

FORBES, ALEXANDER, in Recroy, a soldier in Captain Hugh McLeod of Geanies Independent Company on 17 June 1746. [TGSI.LIII.381]

FORBES, DANIEL, writer in Ribigill, 1747. [NAS.GD84/2/36]

FORBES, DONALD, soldier of Captain George Mackay's Independent Company at Shiromore, 1746. [TGSI.LIII.370]

FORBES, JAMES, in Tain, Easter Ross, 1766. [OR#409]

FORBES, JOHN, a merchant in Tain, Easter Ross, 1766. [OR#408]

FORBES, THOMAS, a tailor in Tain, Easter Ross, 1766. [OR#408]

FORSYTH, ALEXANDER, soldier of Captain Colin Mackenzie's Independent Company, 1746. [TGSI.LIII.385]

FORSYTH, WILLIAM, a merchant in Cromarty, the Black Isle, 13 December 1752. [NAS.RD2.172.543]

FORSYTH, WILLIAM, a linen manufacturer in Cromarty, the Black Isle, during the 1760s. [NAS.E746.95/138]

FOWLER, ALEXANDER, tacksman of Dingwall, Ross and Cromarty, 1767-1773. [NAS.GD46.SEC.1/212]

FOWLER, KENNETH, in Kildinn, soldier of Captain Colin Mackenzie's Independent Company, 1746. [TGSI.LIII.385]

FRASER, ALEXANDER, in Rashell, Applecross, Wester Ross, 1718. [TGSI.LIV.450]

FRASER, ALEXANDER, minister of Avoch, presbytery of Chanonry, 1736 to 1754. [F.7.2]

FRASER, ALEXANDER, with his wife, and two servants, in Clachtole, Assynt, Sutherland, 1774. [SA#74]

FRASER, CHRISTIAN, Lady Applecross, Wester Ross, 1718. [TGSI.LIV.451]

FRASER, DONALD, minister of Killearnan, Ross and Cromarty, from 1744 to 1757. [F.7.12]

FRASER, DONALD, soldier of Captain Hugh McKay's Independent Company, 17 June 1746. [TGSI.LIII.390]

FRASER, DONALD, soldier of Captain George Mackay's Independent Company at Shiromore, 1746. [TGSI.LIII.370]

FRASER, DONALD, a cooper in Tain, Easter Ross, 1766. [OR#408]

FRASER, DONALD, a cottar in Mey, Caithness, 1771. [NAS.GD96.679.14]

FRASER, HECTOR, in Rishell, Applecross, Wester Ross, 1718. [TGSI.LIV.450]

FRASER, HUGH, a cooper in Tain, Easter Ross, 1766. [OR#408]

FRASER, JAMES, born 1695 youngest son of John Fraser of Pitcalzean, Nigg, Easter Ross, educated at King's College, Aberdeen, minister of Alness, Easter Ross, from 1726 to 1769, died 5 October 1769. Husband of Jean, daughter of Donald Macleod of Geanies. [F.7.27]

FRASER, JOHN, born Inverness 1746, son of Simon Fraser, educated at King's College, Aberdeen, minister of Kilmorack from 1769 to 1804, died 4 April 1804. Husband of Margaret Nicolson, parents of Catherine, Mary, Simon, Alexander, and Malcolm. [F.7.39]

FRASER, JOHN, a merchant in the Black Isle, incidents book 1755-1759. [NAS.CS238/misc.29/6]

FRASER, PATRICK, in Dornoch, Sutherland, soldier of Alexander Gunn's Independent Company at Shiromore, 16 June 1746. [TGSI.LIII.368]

FRASER, RONALD, in Corninly, a soldier of the Master of Ross' Independent Company at Linachan, 14 June 1746. [TGSI.LIII.392]

FRASER, SIMON, with his wife, four children, and one servant in Cromauld, Assynt, Sutherland, 1774. [SA#76]

GAIR, JOHN, in Cyderhall, Sutherland, soldier of Alexander Gunn's Independent Company at Shiromore, 16 June 1746. [TGSI.LIII.368]

GAIR, WILLIAM, in Salachie, a soldier of the Master of Ross' Independent Company at Linachan, 14 June 1746. [TGSI.LIII.392]

GALLOWAY, ROBERT, sailor or fisherman settled at New Tarbat, Easter Ross, 1765. [NAS.E746.80]

GEDDES, GEORGE, a cottar in Mey, Caithness, 1771. [NAS.GD96.679.14]

GEDDES, JAMES, tenant in Mill of Mey, Caithness, 1771. [NAS.GD96.679.14]

GEDDES, JOHN, a cottar in Mey, Caithness, 1771. [NAS.GD96.679.14]

GEDDES, WILLIAM, a cottar in Mey, Caithness, 1771. [NAS.GD96.679.14]

GEORGESON, DONALD R., in Tain, Easter Ross, 1766. [OR#409]

GIBSON, ALEXANDER, born 1674 son of Alexander Gibson in Bower. Minister of Canisby, Caithness, from 1705 to 1746 (?). Husband of Margaret Sinclair, and father of John and George. [F.7.117]

GILCHRIST, JAMES, son of John McGilchrist in Kilmichael-Glassary. Minister at Loth, Sutherland, from 1732 to 1738, then at Thurso, Caithness, from 1738 to 1751, died 14 December 1752. Husband of Susanna

Myles and father of Daniel, Margaret, Sarah, William, George, James, Jean, and Dougal [F.7.95/136]

GILLANDERS, ALEXANDER, tacksman of Lochs, Ross and Cromarty, 1773. [NAS.GD46.SEC.1/212]

GILLANDERS, GEORGE, tacksman of Stornaway, Uig, and Lochs, 1765-1776. [NAS.GD46.SEC.1/212]

GORDON, ADAM, Lieutenant of the Munro Independent Company, at Inverness 1745. [MCP.92]

GORDON, ALEXANDER, in Elderbell, soldier of Alexander Gunn's Independent Company at Shiromore, 16 June 1746. [TGSI.LIII.368]

GORDON, ALEXANDER, in Frie, soldier of Alexander Gunn's Independent Company at Shiromore, 16 June 1746. [TGSI.LIII.368]

GORDON, ALEXANDER, in Brick, soldier of Alexander Gunn's Independent Company at Shiromore, 16 June 1746. [TGSI.LIII.368]

GORDON, Lieutenant CHARLES, of Skelpick, tenant farmer, Rientraid, 1766. [SA#67]

GORDON, DONALD, a soldier in Captain Hugh McLeod of Geanies Independent Company on 17 June 1746. [TGSI.LIII.380]

GORDON, GEORGE, minister of Cromarty, the Black Isle, 1707 to 1749, died 28 December 1749. Husband of (1) Mary Forrester, parents of Ann, Janet, Mary, Ann; (2) Jean Moffat. [F.7.5]

GORDON, GEORGE, in Kintradvall, soldier of Alexander Gunn's Independent Company at Shiromore, 16 June 1746. [TGSI.LIII.368]

GORDON, GEORGE, son of George Gordon of Gartly, ordained as minister of Clyne,Sutherland, in 1764, died 2 September 1770. Married Elizabeth, daughter of George

Graham of Drynie, and were parents of Anne born 1765, died 1768, Robert born 1767, and Anne born 1769. [F.7.80]

GORDON, JOHN, Lientenant of the Sutherland Independent Company, at Inverness 1745. [MCP.92]

GORDON, JOHN, in Golspietour, soldier of Alexander Gunn's Independent Company at Shiromore, 16 June 1746. [TGSI.LIII.368]

GORDON, JOHN, in Elderbill, soldier of Alexander Gunn's Independent Company at Shiromore, 16 June 1746. [TGSI.LIII.368]

GORDON, WILLIAM, in Frie, soldier of Alexander Gunn's Independent Company at Shiromore, 16 June 1746. [TGSI.LIII.368]

GOW, GEORGE, in Halladale, Caithness, soldier of Captain Hugh McKay's Independent Company, 17 June 1746. [TGSI.LIII.390]

GOW, HUGH, a soldier of Captain Hugh McKay's Independent Company in 1746. [TGSI.LIII.391]

GOW, JOHN, in Torr, soldier of Captain Hugh McKay's Independent Company, 17 June 1746. [TGSI.LIII.390]

GOW, JOHN, in Dalhabaoy or Dalalva, soldier of Captain Hugh McKay's Independent Company, 17 June 1746. [TGSI.LIII.391]

GOW, JOHN, a tenant in Halladale, Caithness, 1756. [NAS.GD87.SEC2.13]

GRAHAM, ALEXANDER, in Turnack, a soldier of the Master of Ross' Independent Company at Linachan, 14 June 1746. [TGSI.LIII.392]

GRAHAM, ALEXANDER, in Amat, a soldier of the Master of Ross' Independent Company at Linachan, 14 June 1746. [TGSI.LIII.392]

GRAHAM, DONALD, in Amat, a soldier of the Master of Ross' Independent Company at Linachan, 14 June 1746. [TGSI.LIII.392]

GRAHAM, DONALD, tenant in Runabreake, 1770. [NAS.E746.167.5]

GRAHAM, JOHN, tenant in Runabreake, 1770. [NAS.E746.167.5]

GRAHAM, MURDOCH, in Inverack, a soldier of the Master of Ross' Independent Company at Linachan, 14 June 1746. [TGSI.LIII.392]

GRAHAME, ALEXANDER, with his wife, and two servants, in Culkin Drumbeg, Assynt, Sutherland, 1774. [SA#78]

GRAHAME, DONALD, with his wife, and five children, in Culkin Drumbeg, Assynt, Sutherland, 1774. [SA#78]

GRAHAME, DONALD, with his wife, one child, and seven servants, in Drumbeg, Assynt, Sutherland, 1774. [SA#79]

GRAHAME, JOHN, with his wife, one child, and two servants in Culaig, Assynt, Sutherland, 1774. [SA#77]

GRAHAME, JOHN, with his wife, in Unapool, Assynt, Sutherland, 1774. [SA#88]

GRANGE, ROBERT, in Durness, Sutherland, soldier of Captain, Hugh McKay's Independent Company, 17 June 1746. [TGSI.LIII.390]

GRANT, CHRISTIAN, wife of Hector Murray tenant farmer in Mallack, died 1753. [Golspie gravestone, Sutherland]

GRANT, CHRISTIAN, wife of William Grant, died 1766. [Golspie gravestone, Sutherland]

GRANT, DONALD, a sergeant of the Master of Ross' Independent Company at Linachan, 14 June 1746. [TGSI.LIII.391]

GRANT, JAMES, Ensign of the Grant Independent Company, at Inverness 1745. [MCP.92]

GRANT, JOHN, baron baillie for the barony of Coigach, 1757. [NAS.E746.109]

GRANT, MURDOCH, in Lagmacop, Applecross, Wester Ross,, 1718. [TGSI.LIV.450]

GRANT, PATRICK, born 1706, minister of Urray and Tarradale, Ross and Cromarty, from 1749 to 1787, died 14 April 1787. Husband of Anne Spence. [F.7.50]

GRANT, PATRICK, the younger of Rothiemurcus, Lieutenant of the Grant Independent Company, at Inverness 1745. [MCP.92]

GRANT, PATRICK, educated at King's College, Aberdeen, minister of Logie Easter, presbytery of Tain, Easter Ross, from 1744 to 1778, died 19 July 1778. Husband of Anne Grant, parents of Margaret, Anne, Ludovic, Christina (1), Christina (2) James, John, and Marion. [F.7.63]

GRANT, PATRICK, born Cromdale 1715, son of James Grant, minister of Nigg, Easter Ross, from 1756 to 1788, died 19 January 1788. Husband of (1) Isabella Ker, parents of Elizabeth, Andrew, and John; (2) Ann Grant, parents of James, Jean, Anne, Isobel, Sophia, William, Lewis, Patrick, Margaret, and Grizel. [F.7.66]

GRANT, ROBERT, corporal of George Munro of Culcairns' Independent Company, 1745. [TGSI.LIII.364]

GRANT, WILLIAM, possibly the younger of Dellachappel, Lieutenant of the Grant Independent Company, at Inverness 1745. [MCP.92]

GRAY, ALEXANDER, of Overskibo, Sutherland, 1766. [OR#408]

GRAY, ALEXANDER, in Skibo, Sutherland, 1770. [NAS.RD4.208.602]

GRAY, ANDREW, soldier of Captain George Mackay's Independent Company at Shiromore, 1746. [TGSI.LIII.370]

GRAY, JOHN, in Brea, a soldier of the Master of Ross' Independent Company at Linachan, 14 June 1746. [TGSI.LIII.391]

GRAY, JOHN, of Rogart, Sutherland, 1765. [NAS.GD87.Sec.2/18]

GRAY, Lieutenant JOHN, of Elphin, tenant farmer, Unapool, Assynt, Sutherland, 1766, dead by 1774. [SA#67]

GRAY, ROBERT, of Creich, tenant farmer, Ardvar, Glenleraig and Cromalt, Assynt, Sutherland, in 1766 and in 1775. [SA#66/67]

GRAY, SIMON, in Pitarksie, soldier of George Munro of Culcairns' Independent Company, 1745. [TGSI.LIII.364]

GRAY, WILLIAM, born 1687, died 30 April 1746, husband of Janet ... born 1687, died 17 July 1763. [Lairg gravestone, Sutherland]

GREEN, ANDREW, tenant in Eastside of Mey, Caithness, 1771. [NAS.GD96.679.14]

GREEN, PETER, a cottar in Mey, Caithness, 1771. [NAS.GD96.679.14]

GREIG, GEORGE, tacksman of Rosemarkie, the Black Isle, 1774. [NAS.GD46.SEC.1/212]

GRENISH, DONALD, in Knockbean, soldier of Captain Colin Mackenzie's Independent Company, 1746. [TGSI.LIII.384]

GROAT, DONALD, of Warse, 1740. [NAS.GD139.39]

GROAT, DONALD, a cottar in Mey, Caithness, 1771. [NAS.GD96.679.14]

GROAT, HARRY, a cottar in Mey, Caithness, 1771. [NAS.GD96.679.14]

GROAT, JAMES, a cottar in Mey, Caithness, 1771. [NAS.GD96.679.14]

GROAT, KATHERINE, a cottar in Gills, Mey, Caithness, 1771. [NAS.GD96.679.14]

GROAT, MALCOLM, of Warse, factor of Melsetter, 7 July 1752. [NAS.RD4.178/2.67]

GROAT, MALCOLM, portioner of Duncansbay, Caithness, 29 February 1752. [NAS.RD2.178/2]

GROAT, MARY, a cottar in Mey, Caithness, 1771. [NAS.GD96.679.14]

GROAT, ROBERT, a cottar in Gills, Mey, Caithness, 1771. [NAS.GD96.679.14]

GRONE, JAMES, sailor or fisherman settled at New Tarbat, Easter Ross, 1765. [NAS.E746.80]

GUNN, ALEXANDER, of Badenloch, Captain of the Sutherland Independent Company at Inverness 1745, commanded by the Earl of Loudoun at Dornoch, Sutherland, 10 March 1746. [MCP.V.31/93]

GUNN, ALEXANDER, soldier of Captain George Mackay's Independent Company at Shiromore, 1746. [TGSI.LIII.370]

GUNN, ALEXANDER, corporal of Alexander Gunn's Independent Company at Shiromore, 16 June 1746. [TGSI.LIII.369]

GUNN, ALEXANDER, in Knockfin, soldier of Alexander Gunn's Independent Company at Shiromore, 16 June 1746. [TGSI.LIII.368]

GUNN, ALEXANDER, in Borible (1), soldier of Alexander Gunn's Independent Company at Shiromore, 16 June 1746. [TGSI.LIII.368]

GUNN, ALEXANDER, in Borible (2), soldier of Alexander Gunn's Independent Company at Shiromore, 16 June 1746. [TGSI.LIII.368]

GUNN, ALEXANDER, soldier of Captain Colin Mackenzie's Independent Company, 1746. [TGSI.LIII.384]

GUNN, ANGUS, in Craigtown. soldier of Captain Hugh McKay's Independent Company, 17 June 1746. [TGSI.LIII.390]

GUNN, ANGUS, in Skinit, soldier of Captain, Hugh McKay's Independent Company, 17 June 1746. [TGSI.LIII.390]

GUNN, ANGUS, soldier of Captain Hugh McKay's Independent Company, 17 June 1746. [TGSI.LIII.390]

GUNN, ANGUS, in Craigie, soldier of Captain Hugh McKay's Independent Company, 17 June 1746. [TGSI.LIII.390]

GUNN, ANGUS, a tenant in Craigtoun, Halladale, Caithness, 1756. [NAS.GD87.SEC2.13]

GUNN, ARCHIBALD, in Keindonald, soldier of Alexander Gunn's Independent Company at Shiromore, 16 June 1746. [TGSI.LIII.368]

GUNN, DONALD, soldier of Captain George Mackay's Independent Company at Shiromore, 1746. [TGSI.LIII.370]

GUNN, DONALD, in Achintoll, soldier of Alexander Gunn's Independent Company at Shiromore, 16 June 1746. [TGSI.LIII.368]

GUNN, DONALD, in Rea, Caithness, soldier of Alexander Gunn's Independent Company at Shiromore, 16 June 1746. [TGSI.LIII.368]

GUNN, DONALD, in Sandgeo, soldier of Captain Hugh McKay's Independent Company, 17 June 1746. [TGSI.LIII.390]

GUNN, DONALD, in Cargary, soldier of Captain Hugh McKay's Independent Company, 17 June 1746. [TGSI.LIII.390]

GUNN, DONALD, soldier of Captain Colin Mackenzie's Independent Company, 1746. [TGSI.LIII.384]

GUNN, DONALD, a tenant in Halladale, Caithness, 1756. [NAS.GD87.SEC2.13]

GUNN, DONALD, a tenant in Craigtoun, Halladale, Caithness, 1756. [NAS.GD87.SEC2.13]

GUNN, GEORGE, in Badloch, soldier of Alexander Gunn's Independent Company at Shiromore, 16 June 1746. [TGSI.LIII.368]

GUNN, GEORGE, drummer of Alexander Gunn's Independent Company at Shiromore, 16 June 1746. [TGSI.LIII.368]

GUNN, GEORGE, jr., soldier of Captain Hugh McKay's Independent Company, 17 June 1746. [TGSI.LIII.390]

GUNN, HECTOR, piper of Alexander Gunn's Independent Company at Shiromore, 16 June 1746. [TGSI.LIII.368]

GUNN, HUGH, in Scilomy, soldier of Captain Hugh McKay's Independent Company, 17 June 1746. [TGSI.LIII.390]

GUNN, JOHN, soldier of Alexander Gunn's Independent Company at Shiromore, 16 June 1746. [TGSI.LIII.368]

GUNN, JOHN, in Achnichon, soldier of Alexander Gunn's Independent Company at Shiromore, 16 June 1746. [TGSI.LIII.368]

GUNN, JOHN, in Skinit, soldier of Captain Hugh McKay's Independent Company, 17 June 1746. [TGSI.LIII.390]

GUNN, JOHN, a soldier of Captain Hugh McKay's Independent Company in 1746. [TGSI.LIII.391]

GUNN, JOHN, a tenant in Halladale, Caithness, 1756. [NAS.GD87.SEC2.13]

GUNN, WILLIAM, in Torgordstown, soldier of Alexander Gunn's Independent Company at Shiromore, 16 June 1746. [TGSI.LIII.368]

GUNN, WILLIAM, in Achintoll, soldier of Alexander Gunn's Independent Company at Shiromore, 16 June 1746. [TGSI.LIII.368]

GUNN, WILLIAM, in Forsinain, soldier of Captain Hugh McKay's Independent Company, 17 June 1746. [TGSI.LIII.390]

GUNN, WILLIAM, in Auldbrigach, soldier of Alexander Gunn's Independent Company at Shiromore, 16 June 1746. [TGSI.LIII.368]

GUNN, WILLIAM, in Borible, soldier of Alexander Gunn's Independent Company at Shiromore, 16 June 1746. [TGSI.LIII.368]

GUNN, WILLIAM, soldier of Alexander Gunn's Independent Company at Shiromore, 16 June 1746. [TGSI.LIII.368]

GUNN, WILLIAM, in Craigtown, soldier of Captain Hugh McKay's Independent Company, 17 June 1746. [TGSI.LIII.390]

GUNN, WILLIAM, a tenant formerly in Forsinaird then in Islandfornan, in Halladale, Caithness, 1756. [NAS.GD87.SEC2.13]

HAM, JAMES, a cottar in Mey, Caithness, 1771.
[NAS.GD96.679.14]

HARROW, DONALD, tenant in Mey, Caithness, 1771.
[NAS.GD96.679.14]

HARROW, HUGH, tenant in Gills, Mey, Caithness, 1771.
[NAS.GD96.679.14]

HARROW, JOHN, a cottar in Mey, Caithness, 1771.
[NAS.GD96.679.14]

HARPER, GEORGE, a cottar in Mey, Caithness, 1771.
[NAS.GD96.679.14]

HECTORSON, ANGUS, a tenant in Halladale, Caithness, 1756. [NAS.GD87.SEC2.13]

HECTORSON, or MCKENZIE, KENNETH, with his wife, in Clashmore, Assynt, Sutherland, 1774. [SA#75]

HENDERSON, PATRICK, graduated King's College, Aberdeen, 1730-1734, schoolmaster at Golspie, Sutherland, and Auldearn, master of Elgin Grammar School, ordained 1755, minister of Cromarty, the Black Isle, 1755 to 1789, died 6 September 1789. Husband of (1) Elspeth Murray, parents of James, Jean, Margaret, William, Anne, Jean, Elizabeth; (2) Mary Stark, parents of Mary, Jean, Mary, Alexander, George, James (a cabinetmaker who went to Pictou, Nova Scotia), Isobel, James, Arthur, Charles, Mary, Hugh, John, and Catherine. [F.7.6]

HENDERSON, WILLIAM, born 1705, son of John Henderson the schoolmaster of Knockbreck, Durness, Sutherland, minister of Eddrachillis, Sutherland, from 1742 to 1743, died 19 May 1743. [F.3.104]

HENDERSON, WILLIAM, tenant in Gills, Mey, Caithness, 1771. [NAS.GD96.679.14]

HORN, JOHN, tenant in Eastside of Mey, Caithness, 1771. [NAS.GD96.679.14]

HOSSACK, ANGUS, soldier of Captain Hugh McKay's Independent Company, 17 June 1746. [TGSI.LIII.390]

HOSSACK, DONALD, in Obsdale, soldier of George Munro of Culcairns' Independent Company, 1745. [TGSI.LIII.364]

HOSSACK, ISOBEL, tacksman of Rosemarkie, the Black Isle, 1774. [NAS.GD46.SEC.1/212]

HOSSACK, WILLIAM, soldier of Captain Hugh McKay's Independent Company, 17 June 1746. [TGSI.LIII.390]

INGLIS, THOMAS, born 1684, minister of Resolis, Ross and Cromarty, died 27 July 1747. Husband of Anne Urquhart, parents of Anne, Thomas William (who emigrated to Jamaica), Jean, and John. [F.7.19]

INNES, HARRY, of Sandside, Caithness, 1750. [NAS.GD87.Sec.2/12]

INNES, JAMES, tenant in Gills, Mey, Caithness, 1771. [NAS.GD96.679.14]

INNES, JOHN, tenant in Gills, Mey, Caithness, 1771. [NAS.GD96.679.14]

INNES, WILLIAM, of Sandside, Caithness, SC14.78.18/19/20]

JACK, ALEXANDER, tenant in Gills, Mey, Caithness, 1771. [NAS.GD96.679.14]

JACK, WILLIAM, soldier of Captain Alexander Mackenzie's Independent Company, dead by 1746. [TGSI.LIII.383]

JEFFREY, NINIAN, factor for the barony of Coigach, 1764 to 1781. [NAS.E746.75]

JOHNSON, DONALD R., in Tain, Easter Ross, 1766. [OR#409]

JOHNSTON, ALEXANDER, master of the Helen and Margaret of Cromarty, 1742. [NAS.E504.17.1]

JOHNSTON, ALEXANDER, a cottar in Mey, Caithness, 1771. [NAS.GD96.679.14]

JUNOR, ALEXANDER, a mason in Tain, Easter Ross, 1765. [OR#408]

JUNOR, JOHN, a mason in Tain, Easter Ross, 1766. [OR#408]

KELLY, DAVID, in Troternish, a soldier in Captain Hugh McLeod of Geanies Independent Company on 17 June 1746. [TGSI.LIII.380]

KELLY, JOHN, his mother, and a servant, in Auchmore, Assynt, Sutherland, 1774. [SA#72]

KEMP, HARRY, tacksman of Fodderty, 1773. [NAS.GD46.SEC.1/212]

KENNEDY, DOUGALL, sailor or fisherman settled at New Tarbat, Easter Ross, 1765. [NAS.E746.80]

KENNEDY, JOHN, merchant in Knockinnan, 1754. [NAS.GD139.239]

KERR, ALEXANDER, a corporal in Captain Hugh McLeod of Geanies Independent Company on 17 June 1746. [TGSI.LIII.380]

KERR, or MACEAN, ALEXANDER, tenant, with wife and six children, in Achmelvich, Sutherland, 1775. [SA#70]

KERR, ALEXANDER, with his wife, and two children, in Clachtole, Assynt, Sutherland, 1774. [SA#74]

KERR, or MCCURCHY, ALEXANDER, tenant, with wife and five children, and his father, in Achmelvich, Sutherland, 1775. [SA#70]

KERR, ALEXANDER, with five others, in Stoer, Assynt, Sutherland, 1774. [SA#86]

KERR, ANGUS, with his wife, two children and two servants, in Clasnhessie, Assynt, Sutherland, 1774. [SA#76]

KERR, ANGUS, with his wife, and four children, in Drumbeg, Assynt, Sutherland, 1774. [SA#79]

KERR, or MCKILPATRICK, ANGUS, with his wife, and four children, in Lochbannoch, Assynt, Sutherland, 1774. [SA#84]

KERR, ANN, a widow, and four children, in Clachtole, Assynt, Sutherland, 1774. [SA#74]

KERR, CHRISTIAN, a widow, with four children, in Clachtole, Assynt, Sutherland, 1774. [SA#74]

KERR, DONALD, tenant in Runabreake, 1770. [NAS.E746.167.5]

KERR, GATHOLUS, a widower with three children, in Stoer, Assynt, Sutherland, 1774. [SA#86]

KERR, JOHN, in Drumbeug, a soldier in Captain Hugh McLeod of Geanies Independent Company on 17 June 1746. [TGSI.LIII.380]

KERR or MCEAN, JOHN, jr., in Achmelvich, Assynt, Sutherland, 1774. [SA#71]

KERR, JOHN, sr., a carpenter, with his wife, three children and one servant, in Stoer, Assynt, Sutherland, 1774. [SA#86]

KERR, JOHN, jr., with his wife, and six children, in Stoer, Assynt, Sutherland, 1774. [SA#86]

KERR, KENNETH, in Achmelvich, Sutherland, soldier in CapTain, Hugh McLeod of Geanies Independent Company on 17 June 1746. [TGSI.LIII.380]

KERR, KENNETH, tenant, with wife and eight children, in Achmelvich, Assynt, Sutherland, 1774. [SA#70]

KERR, KENNETH, wife, and a servant, in Auchmore, Assynt, Sutherland, 1774. [SA#72]

KERR, KENNETH, with his wife, and three children, in Culkin Drumbeg, Assynt, Sutherland, 1774. [SA#79]

KERR, MARGARET, a widow, with three children, and a servant, in Clachtole, Assynt, Sutherland, 1774. [SA#74]

KERR, MARION, a widow, in Achmelvich, Assynt, Sutherland, 1774. [SA#71]

KERR, MARION, a widow, with three children, in Elphine, Assynt, Sutherland, 1774. [SA#80]

KERR, MARY, a widow and her son, in Achmelvich, Assynt, Sutherland, 1774. [SA#71]

KERR, MURDO, in Store, a soldier in Captain Hugh McLeod of Geanies Independent Company on 17 June 1746. [TGSI.LIII.380]

KERR, MURDO, in Drumbeg, Assynt, Sutherland, 1774. [SA#79]

KERR, MURDO, with his wife, and four children, in Stoer, Assynt, Sutherland, 1774. [SA#86]

KERR, MURDOCH, with his wife, in Clachtole, Assynt, Sutherland, 1774. [SA#74]

KERR, NORMAN, with his wife, and three children, in Lochbannoch, Assynt, Sutherland, 1774. [SA#84]

KERR, NORMAND, in Alfine, a soldier in Captain, Hugh McLeod of Geanies Independent Company on 17 June 1746. [TGSI.LIII.380]

KERR, PETER, in Tain, Easter Ross, 1766. [OR#409]

KERR, RORY, with his wife, and four children, in Stoer, Assynt, Sutherland, 1774. [SA#86]

KILE, JOHN, in Cranark, soldier of Captain, Colin Mackenzie's Independent Company, 1746. [TGSI.LIII.384]

KINLUGAIN, DONALD, in Aldandow, a soldier of the Master of Ross' Independent Company at Linachan, 14 June 1746. [TGSI.LIII.392]

KINLUGGAM, THOMAS, in Gleninuble, a soldier of the Master of Ross' Independent Company at Linachan, 14 June 1746. [TGSI.LIII.391]

KIRK, ROBERT, born 1690 in Aberfoyle, educated at Edinburgh University, minister at Dornoch, Sutherland, 1758, died 27 February 1758, husband of (1) Lillias Sutherland, and (2) Jean Ross, father of seven children, [F.7.84]

LAMOND, or MCLEMIN, NEIL, with his wife, three children, and one servant, in Leadmore, Assynt, Sutherland, 1774. [SA#83]

LEAL, JOHN, a cottar in Mey, Caithness, 1771. [NAS.GD96.679.14]

LEAN, THOMAS R., a shoemaker in Tain, Easter Ross, 1766. [OR#409]

LEBBY, ROBERT, soldier of Captain George Mackay's Independent Company at Shiromore, 1746. [TGSI.LIII.370]

LEITH, ALEXANDER, sailor or fisherman settled at New Tarbat, Easter Ross, 1765. [NAS.E746.80]

LEITH, GEORGE, soldier of Captain George Mackay's Independent Company at Shiromore, dead by 1746. [TGSI.LIII.370]

LEITH, JOHN, master of the Betsy of Wick, Caithness, arrived in Inverness on 31 May 1776 from Kirkcaldy. [NAS.E504.17.4]

LESLIE, JOHN, in Pitarksie, soldier of George Munro of Culcairns' Independent Company, 1745. [TGSI.LIII.364]

LESSLY, ALEXANDER, in Dornoch, Sutherland, soldier of Alexander Gunn's Independent Company at Shiromore, 16 June 1746. [TGSI.LIII.368]

LESSLY, ALEXANDER, in Floth, soldier of Alexander Gunn's Independent Company at Shiromore, 16 June 1746. [TGSI.LIII.369]

LILLIE, DAVID, in Tain, Easter Ross, 1766. [OR#409]

LOGAN, ROBERT, in Pitfuir, soldier of George Munro of Culcairns' Independent Company, 1745. [TGSI.LIII.364]

LUMMIS, JOHN, tacksman of Gillock, 1737. [NAS.GD136.47]

LYON, DONALD, schoolmaster in the barony of Coigach, 1765-1771. [NAS.E746.84]

LYON, JAMES, master of the Adventure of Cromarty, arrived in Inverness on 30 July 1768 from Christiansand, Norway. [NAS.E504.17.4]

MCALLAN, JOHN, in Teskaig, Applecross, Wester Ross, 1718. [TGSI.LIV.451]

MCALLISTER, ANGUS, in Culkein Achnacarnan, Assynt, Sutherland, 1774. [SA#78]

MCALLISTER, ANGUS VICINNASH MCLEOD, with his wife, three children, and one servant in Culaig, Assynt, Sutherland, 1774. [SA#77]

MCALLISTER, DUNCAN VICCOIL, soldier of Captain Alexander Mackenzie's Independent Company, 1746. [TGSI.LIII.382]

MCALLISTER, JOHN, in Barradale, Applecross, Wester Ross, 1718. [TGSI.LIV.451]

MCALLISTER, or MCKENZIE, JOHN, with his wife, child, and three servants, in Clashmore, Assynt, Sutherland, 1774. [SA#75]

MCANDY, ALEXANDER, in Rushell, Applecross, Wester Ross, 1718. [TGSI.LIV.450]

MCANGUS, or MACKAY, JOHN, a tenant in Halladale, Caithness, 1756. [NAS.GD87.SEC2.13]

MCANGUS, JOHN, a tenant in Halladale, Caithness, 1756. [NAS.GD87.SEC2.13]

MCANGUS, ROBERT, a tenant in Halladale, Caithness, 1756. [NAS.GD87.SEC2.13]

MCARTHUR, JOHN, minister of Logie Easter, presbytery of Tain, Easter Ross, from 1730 to 1744, died 23 March 1744. Husband of Katherine Fraser. [F.7.63]

MCAULAY, ANGUS, tenant in Badentarbert, 1770. [NAS.E746.167.4]

MCAULAY, AULAY, in Auchindrean, 1758. [NAS.E746.155]

MACAYE, ANGUS, soldier of Captain Alexander Mackenzie's Independent Company, 1746. [TGSI.LIII.383]

MACAYE, DUNCAN, in Salchy, soldier of Captain Alexander Mackenzie's Independent Company, 1746. [TGSI.LIII.382]

MACAYE, DUNCAN, in Glenlum, soldier of Captain Alexander Mackenzie's Independent Company, 1746. [TGSI.LIII.383]

MACAYE, DUNCAN, in Achmore, soldier of Captain Alexander Mackenzie's Independent Company, 1746. [TGSI.LIII.383]

MACAYE, JOHN, in Ardnarff, soldier of Captain Alexander Mackenzie's Independent Company, 1746. [TGSI.LIII.383]

MCBAIN, JOHN, a tailor in Tain, Easter Ross, 1766. [OR#408]

MCBEATH, ALEXANDER, in Frie, soldier of Alexander Gunn's Independent Company at Shiromore, 16 June 1746. [TGSI.LIII.369]

MCBEATH, JOHN, in Frie, soldier of Alexander Gunn's Independent Company at Shiromore, 16 June 1746. [TGSI.LIII.369]

MCBEATH, JOHN, servant of John Sinclair of Freswick, Caithness, 1766. [NAS.GD139.231]

MCBEATH, JOHN, a cottar in Mey, Caithness, 1771. [NAS.GD96.679.14]

MCBEATH, RODERICK, in Frie, soldier of Alexander Gunn's Independent Company at Shiromore, 16 June 1746. [TGSI.LIII.369]

MCBEATH, WILLIAM, tenant in Longoe, Mey, Caithness, 1771. [NAS.GD96.679.14]

MCBEATH, WILLIAM, tenant in Eastside of Mey, Caithness, 1771. [NAS.GD96.679.14]

MCBETH, WILLIAM, sergeant of Alexander Gunn's Independent Company at Shiromore, 16 June 1746. [TGSI.LIII.369]

MCCALLIE, WILLIAM, a weaver in Tain, Easter Ross, 1766. [OR#409]

MCCALOCH, HUGH, in Davoch, soldier of Captain Colin Mackenzie's Independent Company, 1746. [TGSI.LIII.384]

MCCASKILL, ANGUS, with his wife, and one servant, in Lochbannoch, Assynt, Sutherland, 1774. [SA#84]

MCCASKILL, DONALD, with his brother, mother, two sisters, and grandmother, in Culkein Achnacarnan, Assynt, Sutherland, 1774. [SA#78]

MCCASKILL, DONALD, with his wife, and seven children, in Lochbannoch, Assynt, Sutherland, 1774. [SA#84]

MCCASKILL, HUGH, in Duchlash, Assynt, Sutherland, 1774. [SA#80]

MCCASKILL, HUGH, with his wife, three children and one servant, in Polgarvir, Assynt, Sutherland, 1774. [SA#86]

MCCASKILL, WILLIAM, with his wife, two children and one servant, in Polgarvir, Assynt, Sutherland, 1774. [SA#86]

MCCHAVICH, DONALD ROY, soldier of Captain Alexander Mackenzie's Independent Company, 1746. [TGSI.LIII.382]

MCCHAVICH, DUNCAN, soldier of Captain Alexander Mackenzie's Independent Company, 1746. [TGSI.LIII.382]

MCCHONDRY, JOHN, in Innesheal, soldier of Captain Colin Mackenzie's Independent Company, 1746. [TGSI.LIII.384]

MCCOMAS, HUGH, a tenant in Forsinard, Halladale, Caithness, 1756. [NAS.GD87.SEC2.13]

MCCONACHY, ALEXANDER, in Auchnadroil, Applecross, Wester Ross,, 1718. [TGSI.LIV.451]

MCCONACHY, ANGUS, in Barradale, Applecross, Wester Ross,, 1718. [TGSI.LIV.451]

MCCONACHY, PHILIP, in Achachork, Applecross, Wester Ross,, 1718. [TGSI.LIV.452]

MCCONCHY, MURDOCH, in Balbaer, soldier of Captain Colin Mackenzie's Independent Company, 1746. [TGSI.LIII.384]

MCCONEL, WILLIAM, in Borrodale, Applecross, Wester Ross,, 1718. [TGSI.LIV.451]

MCCONN, HUGH, a tenant in Halladale, Caithness, 1756. [NAS.GD87.SEC2.13]

MCCORMAT, ALEXANDER, in Lagmacop, Applecross, Wester Ross,, 1718. [TGSI.LIV.450]

MCCOULL, ALEXANDER, in Forsinain, soldier of Captain Hugh McKay's Independent Company, 17 June 1746. [TGSI.LIII.390]

MCCOULL, ALEXANDER, in Corkall, soldier of Captain Hugh McKay's Independent Company, 17 June 1746. [TGSI.LIII.390]

MCCOULL, HUGH, a tenant in Halladale, Caithness, 1756. [NAS.GD87.SEC2.13]

MCCOULL, HUGH, a tenant in Dalalvah, Halladale, Caithness, 1756. [NAS.GD87.SEC2.13]

MCCOULL, JOHN, in Dispolly, soldier of Captain Hugh McKay's Independent Company, 17 June 1746. [TGSI.LIII.390]

MCCOULL, JOHN, in Corkhall, soldier of Captain Hugh McKay's Independent Company, 17 June 1746. [TGSI.LIII.390]

MCCOULL, JOSEPH, soldier of Captain Hugh McKay's Independent Company, 17 June 1746. [TGSI.LIII.390]

MCCOULL, NIEL, in Tailer, a soldier of Captain Hugh McKay's Independent Company in 1746. [TGSI.LIII.391]

MACCRA, ANN, a widow, two children, and two servants, in Pollakarkan, Auchmore, Assynt, Sutherland, 1774. [SA#72]

MCCRA, DONALD, with his wife, one child, and one servant, in Glenlerag, Assynt, Sutherland, 1774. [SA#80]

MCCRAE, ALEXANDER, with his wife, two children, and two servants, in Glenlerag, Assynt, Sutherland, 1774. [SA#80]

MCCRAE, DONALD, a weaver in Tain, Easter Ross, 1766. [OR#409]

MCCULLOCH, ALEXANDER, a merchant in Tain, Easter Ross, 1752. [NAS.RD4.178/1.161]

MCCULLOCH, ANDREW, in Dornoch, Sutherland, soldier of Alexander Gunn's Independent Company at Shiromore, 16 June 1746. [TGSI.LIII.369]

MCCULLOCH, DUNCAN, in Tronimbrass, Applecross, Wester Ross,, 1718. [TGSI.LIV.450]

MCCULLOCH, GEORGE, born 1728 in the Black Isle, educated at Marischal College, a schoolmaster at Golspie, Sutherland, the minister of Loth, Sutherland, from 1756 to 1800, died 27 December 1800, husband of Elizabeth Forbes, parents of thirteen children. [F.7.96]

MCCULLOCH, HUGH, in Invereathie, Tain, Easter Ross, 1766. [OR#409]

MCCULLOCH, KENNETH, farmer in Allerton, parish of Cromarty, the Black Isle, 1766. [NAS.E746.137]

MCCURCHY, ALEXANDER, and his mother, four children, and a servant, at Ardvar, Assynt, Sutherland, 1774. [SA#72]

MCCURCHY, or MCKENZIE, JOHN, with his wife, and one servant, in Clashmore, Assynt, Sutherland, 1774. [SA#75]

MCCURCHY, MURDOCH, in Culkin Drumbeg, Assynt, Sutherland, 1774. [SA#78]

MCCURICHIE, DONALD BAYNE, in Tain, Easter Ross, 1766. [OR#409]

MCDAVD, ALEXANDER, in Kincraig, a soldier in Captain Hugh McLeod of Geanies Independent Company on 17 June 1746. [TGSI.LIII.381]

MACDONALD, ALEXANDER, in Pitfuir, soldier of George Munro of Culcairns' Independent Company, 1745. [TGSI.LIII.364]

MCDONALD, ALEXANDER, in Balinerige, soldier of Captain Colin Mackenzie's Independent Company, 1746. [TGSI.LIII.384]

MCDONALD, ALEXANDER, with his wife, and two children, in Glenlerag, Assynt, Sutherland, 1774. [SA#80]

MCDONALD, ALEXANDER, in Layne, Assynt, Sutherland, 1774. [SA#85]

MCDONALD, ALEXANDER, with his wife, and four children, in Stronchrubie, Assynt, Sutherland, 1774. [SA#87]

MCDONALD, ANGUS, in Garvade, soldier of Captain Colin Mackenzie's Independent Company, 1746. [TGSI.LIII.385]

MCDONALD, ANGUS, with his wife, child, and servant, in Clasnhessie, Assynt, Sutherland, 1774. [SA#76]

MACDONALD, ANN, schoolmistress in Golspie, died in January 1766. [Golspie gravestone, Sutherland]

MCDONALD, ANN, a widow with two children, in Stronchubie, Assynt, Sutherland, 1774. [SA#87]

MCDONALD, ARCHIBALD, in Lairg, a soldier of the Master of Ross' Independent Company at Linachan, 14 June 1746. [TGSI.LIII.391]

MCDONALD, or GAULD, DAVID, in Tain, Easter Ross, 1766. [OR#409]

MCDONALD, DONALD, with two servants, in Achnacarnan, Assynt, Sutherland, 1774. [SA#72]

MCDONALD, DONALD, with his wife, and two children, in Clasnhessie, Assynt, Sutherland, 1774. [SA#76]

MCDONALD, DONALD, with his wife, and six children, in Culin, Kirkton, Assynt, Sutherland, 1774. [SA#82]

MCDONALD, DONALD, a grasskeeper, with his son, in Torbreck, Assynt, Sutherland, 1774. [SA#87]

MACDONALD, DUNCAN, in Salchie, soldier of George Munro of Culcairns' Independent Company, 1745. [TGSI.LIII.364]

MCDONALD, EVAN, in Inverchasley, a soldier of the Master of Ross' Independent Company at Linachan, 14 June 1746. [TGSI.LIII.391]

MCDONALD, HUGH, tenant in Badentarbert, 1770. [NAS.E746.167.4]

MCDONALD, JOHN, in Borrodale, Applecross, Wester Ross,, 1718. [TGSI.LIV.451]

MCDONALD, JOHN, in Ledmore, a soldier in Captain Hugh McLeod of Geanies Independent Company on 17 June 1746. [TGSI.LIII.380]

MCDONALD, JOHN, piper of Captain Hugh McKay's Independent Company in 1746. [TGSI.LIII.389]

MCDONALD, JOHN, in Drumsordlan, a soldier in Captain Hugh McLeod of Geanies Independent Company on 17 June 1746. [TGSI.LIII.380]

MACDONALD, JOHN, in Achindreat, soldier of Captain Colin Mackenzie's Independent Company, 1746. [TGSI.LIII.384]

MCDONALD, JOHN, with his wife, and five children, in Ardvar, Assynt, Sutherland, 1774. [SA#73]

MCDONALD, JOHN, with his wife, and child, in Culkein Achnacarnan, Assynt, Sutherland, 1774. [SA#78]

MCDONALD, JOHN, with his wife, and two children, in Leadmore, Assynt, Sutherland, 1774. [SA#83]

MCDONALD, JOHN OAG, with his wife, and one servant, in Stronchrubie, Assynt, Sutherland, 1774. [SA#87]

MCDONALD, MURDO, and four of a family, in Nedd, Assynt, Sutherland, 1774. [SA#85]

MACDONALD, MURDOCH, born 1696 son of Donald MacDonald in Durness, Sutherland, graduated MA from St Andrews in 1722, minister of Durness from 1726 to 1763, died on 23 August 1763, husband of Anna Coupar, parents of eleven children. [F.7.102]

MCDONALD, MURDOCH, in Luberoy, a soldier of the Master of Ross' Independent Company at Linachan, 14 June 1746. [TGSI.LIII.392]

MCDONALD, NORMAND, wife, child and a servant, in Achmore, Assynt, Sutherland, 1774. [SA#71]

MCDONALD, ROBERT, with his wife, and two children, in Ardvar, Assynt, Sutherland, 1774. [SA#73]

MACDONALD, THOMAS, in Pitarksie, soldier of George Munro of Culcairns' Independent Company, 1745. [TGSI.LIII.364]

MACDONALD, WILLIAM, soldier of George Munro of Culcairns' Independent Company, 1745. [TGSI.LIII.364]

MACDONALD, WILLIAM, the elder, in Pitfuir, soldier of George Munro of Culcairns' Independent Company, 1745. [TGSI.LIII.364]

MACDONALD, WILLIAM, soldier of George Munro of Culcairns' Independent Company, 1745. [TGSI.LIII.364]

MACDONALD, WILLIAM, the younger, in Pitfuir, soldier of George Munro of Culcairns' Independent Company, 1745. [TGSI.LIII.364]

MCDONALD, WILLIAM, in Achvriell, soldier of Alexander Gunn's Independent Company at Shiromore, 16 June 1746. [TGSI.LIII.369]

MCDONALD, WILLIAM, soldier of Alexander Gunn's Independent Company at Shiromore, 16 June 1746. [TGSI.LIII.369]

MCDOUGALL, ANDREW, sailor or fisherman settled at New Tarbat, Easter Ross, 1765. [NAS.E746.80]

MACEACHIN, or MACKENZIE, ALEXANDER, in Arteaskley, Applecross, Wester Ross, 1718. [TGSI.LIV.452]

MCEACHIN, COLLIN, in Barradale, Applecross, Wester Ross,, 1718. [TGSI.LIV.451]

MACEACHIN, JOHN, in Sheldack, Applecross, Wester Ross,, 1718. [TGSI.LIV.452]

MCEAN, ALEXANDER VICALISTER, in Rishell, Applecross, Wester Ross, 1718. [TGSI.LIV.450]

MCEAN, ALEXANDER OIGE, in Belnain, soldier of Captain Colin Mackenzie's Independent Company, 1746. [TGSI.LIII.385]

MCEAN, DONALD, in Borrodale, Applecross, Wester Ross, 1718. [TGSI.LIV.451]

MCEAN, DONALD VICINISH VICCANMORE, in Rashell, Applecross, Wester Ross, 1718. [TGSI.LIV.450]

MCEAN, DONALD VICUNLEY, in Cullnokill, Applecross, Wester Ross, 1718. [TGSI.LIV.452]

MCEAN, DUNCAN, in Lagmacop, Applecross, Wester Ross, 1718. [TGSI.LIV.450]

MCEAN, DUNCAN, in Borrodale, Applecross, Wester Ross, 1718. [TGSI.LIV.451]

MCEAN, or MCKENZIE, JAMES, with his wife, two children and one servant, in Unapool, Assynt, Sutherland, 1774. [SA#88]

MCEAN, JAMES EER, in Belnain, soldier of Captain Colin Mackenzie's Independent Company, 1746. [TGSI.LIII.385]

MCEAN, JOHN BAYN, in Eyr, soldier of Captain Alexander Mackenzie's Independent Company, 1746. [TGSI.LIII.382]

MCEAN, KENNETH, in Eyr, soldier of Captain Alexander Mackenzie's Independent Company, 1746. [TGSI.LIII.382]

MCEAN, or MCKENZIE, MURDOCH, with his wife and three children, in Ardvar, Assynt, Sutherland, 1774. [SA#72]

MCEAN, RORY, in Rushill, Applecross, Wester Ross, 1718. [TGSI.LIV.450]

MCEAN, RORY, in Lagginteamore, Applecross, Wester Ross, 1718. [TGSI.LIV.450]

MCEAN, RORY, in Borrodale, Applecross, Wester Ross, 1718. [TGSI.LIV.451]

MCEAN, RORY VICURCHY, in Achachork, Applecross, Wester Ross, 1718. [TGSI.LIV.452]

MCEAN, RORY VICUNLEY, in Cullnokill, Applecross, Wester Ross, 1718. [TGSI.LIV.452]

MCEAN, RORY, with his wife, two children, and four children, and one servant in Culaig, Assynt, Sutherland, 1774. [SA#77]

MCEANEER, JAMES, in Belnain, soldier of Captain Colin Mackenzie's Independent Company, 1746. [TGSI.LIII.385]

MCEUAN, ALEXANDER, in Lagmacop, Applecross, Wester Ross, 1718. [TGSI.LIV.450]

MCEVAN, JOHN, in Polisky, soldier of George Munro of Culcairns' Independent Company, 1745. [TGSI.LIII.364]

MACEVAR, ALEXANDER, in Brahan, soldier of Captain Colin Mackenzie's Independent Company, 1746. [TGSI.LIII.385]

MACEVAR, JOHN, corporal of Captain Colin Mackenzie's Independent Company, 1746. [TGSI.LIII.384]

MCEWER, MURDOCH, tenant in Dornie, 1770. [NAS.E746.167.4]

MCEWER, RODERICK, with his wife, and two children, in Clashmore, Assynt, Sutherland, 1774. [SA#75]

MCFARQUHAR, DUNCAN, in Ardachie, Applecross, Wester Ross, 1718. [TGSI.LIV.451]

MCFARQUHAR, FINLAY, in Auchnadroil, Applecross, Wester Ross, 1718. [TGSI.LIV.451]

MACFARQUHAR, H., in Tain, Easter Ross, 1766. [OR#408]

MCFARQUHAR, JOHN, in Ardachie, Applecross, Wester Ross, 1718. [TGSI.LIV.451]

MCFINLAY, DONALD, in Langwell, Applecross, Wester Ross, 1718. [TGSI.LIV.451]

MCFINLAY, JOHN, in Knockbean, soldier of Captain Colin Mackenzie's Independent Company, 1746. [TGSI.LIII.384]

MCFINLAY, or MCCRA, LACHLAN, with his wife, two children, and one servant, in Nedd, Assynt, Sutherland, 1774. [SA#85]

MCGILLESPICK, ALEXANDER, in Cullnokill, Applecross, Wester Ross, 1718. [TGSI.LIV.452]

MCGILLESPICK, ANGUS, in Barradale, Applecross, Wester Ross, 1718. [TGSI.LIV.451]

MCGILLESPICK, JOHN, in Achachork, Applecross, Wester Ross, 1718. [TGSI.LIV.452]

MCGILLICHALLUM, JOHN, in Langwell, Applecross, Wester Ross, 1718. [TGSI.LIV.451]

MACGILLICHRIST, MURDOCH, in Ballogie, Applecross, Wester Ross, 1718. [TGSI.LIV.452]

MACGILLICHRIST, NORMAND, in Ballogie, Applecross, Wester Ross, 1718. [TGSI.LIV.452]

MCGRIGOR or MCLEOD, MURDOCH, tenant in Badintarbert, 1758. [NAS.E746.113.14]

MCGRUMAN, JOHN, sergeant of Captain Colin Mackenzie's Independent Company, 1746. [TGSI.LIII.384]

MCHOMAS, DONALD R., a weaver in Tain, Easter Ross, 1766. [OR#409]

MCHOMASH, DONALD, miller at the Mill of Oldney, Assynt, Sutherland, with four children, 1774. [SA#85]

MCHOMASH, THOMAS, a weaver in Tain, Easter Ross, 1766. [OR#409]

MCHUTCHEON, or MCLEOD, ALEXANDER, with his wife, two children, and one servant, in Knockan, Assynt, Sutherland, 1774. [SA#83]

MCHUTCHEON, JOHN, in Culkin Drumbeg, Assynt, Sutherland, 1774. [SA#78]

MCINISH, JOHN, in Auchnadroil, Applecross, Wester Ross, 1718. [TGSI.LIV.451]

MCINNES, ALEXANDER, soldier of Captain Alexander Mackenzie's Independent Company, 1746. [TGSI.LIII.383]

MCINNES, DONALD, in Achmelvich, Assynt, Sutherland, 1774. [SA#71]

MCINNES, JOHN, sr., soldier of Captain Alexander Mackenzie's Independent Company, 1746. [TGSI.LIII.383]

MCINNES, JOHN, jr., soldier of Captain Alexander Mackenzie's Independent Company, 1746. [TGSI.LIII.383]

MCINNES, or MCLEOD, NORMAND, with his wife, and six children, in Culkein Achnacarnan, Assynt, Sutherland, 1774. [SA#78]

MCINTEIR, JOHN, soldier of Captain Alexander Mackenzie's Independent Company, 1746. [TGSI.LIII.382]

MACINTOSH, ALEXANDER, soldier of Captain George Mackay's Independent Company at Shiromore, 1746. [TGSI.LIII.371]

MCINTOSH, ANDREW, a soldier of the Master of Ross' Independent Company at Linachan, 14 June 1746. [TGSI.LIII.392]

MCINTOSH, DONALD, in Dalnumein, soldier of Alexander Gunn's Independent Company at Shiromore, 16 June 1746. [TGSI.LIII.369]

MCINTOSH, GEORGE, in Newmore, a soldier in Captain Hugh McLeod of Geanies Independent Company on 17 June 1746. [TGSI.LIII.381]

MACINTOSH, GEORGE, soldier of Captain George Mackay's Independent Company at Shiromore, 1746. [TGSI.LIII.371]

MCINTOSH, GEORGE, soldier of Captain Hugh McKay's Independent Company, 17 June 1746. [TGSI.LIII.391]

MCINTOSH, HUGH, in Reroy, soldier of Captain Hugh McKay's Independent Company, 17 June 1746. [TGSI.LIII.391]

MACINTOSH, HUGH, in Kylestrome, soldier of Captain George Mackay's Independent Company at Shiromore, 1746. [TGSI.LIII.371]

MACINTOSH, HUGH, in Eribol, soldier of Captain George Mackay's Independent Company at Shiromore, 1746. [TGSI.LIII.371]

MACINTOSH, HUGH, in Durness, soldier of Captain George Mackay's Independent Company at Shiromore, 1746. [TGSI.LIII.371]

MCINTOSH, JAMES, in Dalnumein, soldier of Alexander Gunn's Independent Company at Shiromore, 16 June 1746. [TGSI.LIII.369]

MCINTOSH, JOHN, in Pitarskie, soldier of George Munro of Culcairns' Independent Company, 1745. [TGSI.LIII.364]

MCINTOSH, MARY, with her mother and grandchild, in Inverkirkaig, Assynt, Sutherland, 1774. [SA#82]

MCINTOSH, MURDO, soldier of Captain Alexander Mackenzie's Independent Company, 1746. [TGSI.LIII.382]

MCINTOSH, MURDOCH, a soldier of Captain Hugh McKay's Independent Company in 1746. [TGSI.LIII.391]

MCINTOSH, RORIE, soldier of Captain Alexander Mackenzie's Independent Company, 1746. [TGSI.LIII.382]

MCIVER, ALEXANDER, master of the Adventure of Cromarty, arrived in Inverness on 14 May 1769 from Sunderland, England. [NAS.E504.17.4]

MCIVER, ANGUS, master of the Adventure of Cromarty, arrived in Inverness on 2 January 1766 from Newcastle, England. [NAS.E504.17.3]

MCIVER, JOHN, soldier of Captain Alexander Mackenzie's Independent Company, 1746. [TGSI.LIII.382]

MCIVER, JOHN, soldier of Captain Colin Mackenzie's Independent Company, 1746. [TGSI.LIII.384]

MCIVER, JOHN, with his wife, four children, in Glenlerag, Assynt, Sutherland, 1774. [SA#80]

MCKAY, ALEXANDER, born 1698, died 1770. [Gairloch gravestone, Wester Ross]

MACKAY, ALEXANDER, in Pitfuir, soldier of George Munro of Culcairns' Independent Company, 1745. [TGSI.LIII.364]

MCKAY, ALEXANDER, in Achellia, soldier of Alexander Gunn's Independent Company at Shiromore, 16 June 1746. [TGSI.LIII.369]

MCKAY, ALEXANDER, in Balvraid, soldier of Alexander Gunn's Independent Company at Shiromore, 16 June 1746. [TGSI.LIII.369]

MCKAY, ALEXANDER, in Skelbo, soldier of Alexander Gunn's Independent Company at Shiromore, 16 June 1746. [TGSI.LIII.369]

MACKAY, ALEXANDER, in Kylestrome, soldier of Captain George Mackay's Independent Company at Shiromore, 1746. [TGSI.LIII.370]

MACKAY, ALEXANDER, in Borgie, soldier of Captain George Mackay's Independent Company at Shiromore, 1746. [TGSI.LIII.370]

MACKAY, ALEXANDER, in Cloionell, soldier of Captain George Mackay's Independent Company at Shiromore, 1746. [TGSI.LIII.371]

MACKAY, ALEXANDER, in Kinloch, soldier of Captain George Mackay's Independent Company at Shiromore, dead by 1746. [TGSI.LIII.371]

MACKAY, ALEXANDER, in Strathmelness, soldier of Captain George Mackay's Independent Company at Shiromore, dead by 1746. [TGSI.LIII.371]

MACKAY, ALEXANDER, in Farr, Sutherland, soldier of Captain George Mackay's Independent Company at Shiromore, dead by 1746. [TGSI.LIII.371]

MCKAY, ALL., in Salach, a soldier of the Master of Ross' Independent Company at Linachan, 14 June 1746. [TGSI.LIII.391]

MCKAY, ALL., in Tormilich, a soldier of the Master of Ross' Independent Company at Linachan, 14 June 1746. [TGSI.LIII.391]

MCKAY, ANGUS, in Layne, a soldier in Captain Hugh McLeod of Geanies Independent Company on 17 June 1746. [TGSI.LIII.380]

MACKAY, ANGUS, in Maldy, soldier of Captain George Mackay's Independent Company at Shiromore, 1746. [TGSI.LIII.370]

MACKAY, ANGUS, in Ribbigily, soldier of Captain George Mackay's Independent Company at Shiromore, 1746. [TGSI.LIII.370]

MACKAY, ANGUS, in Kylestrome, soldier of Captain George Mackay's Independent Company at Shiromore, 1746. [TGSI.LIII.370]

MCKAY, ANGUS, drummer of Captain Hugh McKay's Independent Company in 1746. [TGSI.LIII.389]

MCKAY, ANGUS, soldier of Alexander Gunn's Independent Company at Shiromore, 16 June 1746. [TGSI.LIII.369]

MCKAY, ANGUS, in Skinnet, soldier of Captain Hugh McKay's Independent Company, 17 June 1746. [TGSI.LIII.391]

NCKAY, Mrs BETSY, born 1724, died on 10 May 1758, wife of Hugh McKay of Kylestrome, and daughter of John Mackay of Mudale. [Kylestrome gravestone, Sutherland]

MACKAY, CHARLES, soldier of Captain George Mackay's Independent Company at Shiromore, dead by 1746. [TGSI.LIII.371]

MCKAY, DANIEL, in Invercharin, a soldier of the Master of Ross' Independent Company at Linachan, 14 June 1746. [TGSI.LIII.392]

MACKAY, DONALD, of Clashneach, 1740. [NAS.GD84/2/23]

MACKAY, DONALD, drummer of George Munro of Culcairns' Independent Company, 1745. [TGSI.LIII.364]

MACKAY, DONALD, in Auchany, soldier of George Munro of Culcairns' Independent Company, 1745. [TGSI.LIII.364]

MCKAY, DONALD, (1), corporal of Captain Hugh McKay's Independent Company in 1746. [TGSI.LIII.389]

MCKAY, DONALD, (2), corporal of Captain Hugh McKay's Independent Company died in 1746. [TGSI.LIII.389]

MCKAY, DONALD, in Sartigrim, soldier of Captain Hugh McKay's Independent Company, 17 June 1746. [TGSI.LIII.390]

MACKAY, DONALD, in Eribol, soldier of Captain George Mackay's Independent Company at Shiromore, dead by 1746. [TGSI.LIII.370]

MCKAY, DONALD, in Hevagmore, soldier of Captain Hugh McKay's Independent Company, 17 June 1746. [TGSI.LIII.390]

MCKAY, DONALD, a soldier of Captain Hugh McKay's Independent Company in 1746. [TGSI.LIII.391]

MCKAY, DONALD, in Forsinard, soldier of Captain Hugh McKay's Independent Company, 17 June 1746. [TGSI.LIII.390]

MCKAY, DONALD, in Hope, soldier of Captain Hugh McKay's Independent Company, 17 June 1746. [TGSI.LIII.390]

MACKAY, DONALD, in Baddveoir, soldier of Captain George Mackay's Independent Company at Shiromore, 1746. [TGSI.LIII.371]

MACKAY, DONALD, in Durin, soldier of Captain George Mackay's Independent Company at Shiromore, 1746. [TGSI.LIII.371]

MACKAY, DONALD, in Oldshours, soldier of Captain George Mackay's Independent Company at Shiromore, dead by 1746. [TGSI.LIII.371]

MCKAY, DONALD, in Island Roan, soldier of Captain Hugh McKay's Independent Company, 17 June 1746. [TGSI.LIII.390]

MACKAY, DONALD, in Sandwood, soldier of Captain George Mackay's Independent Company at Shiromore, dead by 1746. [TGSI.LIII.371]

MCKAY, DONALD, in Aladoll, a soldier of the Master of Ross' Independent Company at Linachan, 14 June 1746. [TGSI.LIII.391]

MACKAY, DONALD, in Skerray, soldier of Captain George Mackay's Independent Company at Shiromore, 1746. [TGSI.LIII.370]

MACKAY, DONALD, in Strathmore, soldier of Captain George Mackay's Independent Company at Shiromore, dead by 1746. [TGSI.LIII.371]

MACKAY, DONALD, a tenant in Halladale, Caithness, 1756. [NAS.GD87.SEC2.13]

MACKAY, DONALD, a merchant in Thurso, Caithness, an account book 1768 -1770. [NAS.CS235/M7/5]

MACKAY, FINLAY, soldier of Captain George Mackay's Independent Company at Shiromore, dead by 1746. [TGSI.LIII.370]

MACKAY, GEORGE, born 1713 son of John Mackay; minister of Eddrachillis, Sutherland, died 18 June 1741. [F.7.104]

MACKAY, GEORGE, of Skibo, Sutherland, Captain of an Independent Company commanded by the Earl of Loudoun at Inverness 1745, at Dornoch, Sutherland, 10 March 1746. [MCP.V.31/92]; 1752. [NAS.RD2.171/2.384]

MCKAY, GEORGE, in Tongue, Sutherland, soldier of Captain Hugh McKay's Independent Company, 17 June 1746. [TGSI.LIII.391]

MACKAY, GEORGE, in Tongue, Sutherland, soldier of Captain George Mackay's Independent Company at Shiromore, 1746. [TGSI.LIII.370]

MCKAY, GEORGE, in Torisdale, soldier of Captain Hugh McKay's Independent Company, 17 June 1746. [TGSI.LIII.390]

MACKAY, GEORGE, in Sleisdaridh, soldier of Captain George Mackay's Independent Company at Shiromore, 1746. [TGSI.LIII.371]

MCKAY, GEORGE, in Kiendonald, soldier of Alexander Gunn's Independent Company at Shiromore, 16 June 1746. [TGSI.LIII.369]

MCKAY, GEORGE, in Forsinaird, soldier of Captain Hugh McKay's Independent Company, 17 June 1746. [TGSI.LIII.390]

MACKAY, HECTOR, in Island Roan, soldier of Captain George Mackay's Independent Company at Shiromore, 1746. [TGSI.LIII.370]

MACKAY, HECTOR, in Scrabster, soldier of Captain George Mackay's Independent Company at Shiromore, 1746. [TGSI.LIII.371]

MACKAY, HUGH, of Bighouse, Captain of an Independent Company commanded by the Earl of Loudoun at Dornoch, 10 March 1746. [MCP.V.31]

MCKAY, HUGH, in Newmore, a soldier in Captain Hugh McLeod of Geanies Independent Company on 17 June 1746. [TGSI.LIII.380]

MACKAY, HUGH, in Eribol, soldier of Captain George Mackay's Independent Company at Shiromore, 1746. [TGSI.LIII.371]

MACKAY, HUGH, sergeant of Captain George Mackay's Independent Company at Shiromore, 1746. [TGSI.LIII.370]

MACKAY, HUGH, corporal of Captain George Mackay's Independent Company at Shiromore, 1746. [TGSI.LIII.370]

MCKAY, HUGH, corporal of Captain Hugh McKay's Independent Company in 1746. [TGSI.LIII.389]

MCKAY, HUGH, in Bighouse, soldier of Captain Hugh McKay's Independent Company, 17 June 1746. [TGSI.LIII.390]

MCKAY, HUGH, in Forsinaird, soldier of Captain Hugh McKay's Independent Company, 17 June 1746. [TGSI.LIII.390]

MCKAY, HUGH, in Tailor, soldier of Captain Hugh McKay's Independent Company, 17 June 1746. [TGSI.LIII.390]

MACKAY, HUGH, in Huinleam, soldier of Captain George Mackay's Independent Company at Shiromore, 1746. [TGSI.LIII.370]

MCKAY, HUGH, in Breckruw, soldier of Captain Hugh McKay's Independent Company, 17 June 1746. [TGSI.LIII.390]

MACKAY, HUGH, in Ardachow, soldier of Captain George Mackay's Independent Company at Shiromore, 1746. [TGSI.LIII.370]

MCKAY, HUGH, in Scoury, soldier of Captain Hugh McKay's Independent Company, 17 June 1746. [TGSI.LIII.390]

MCKAY, HUGH, in Reantle, soldier of Captain Hugh McKay's Independent Company, 17 June 1746. [TGSI.LIII.390]

MACKAY, HUGH, in Maldy, soldier of Captain George Mackay's Independent Company at Shiromore, 1746. [TGSI.LIII.370]

MACKAY, HUGH, in Brae Tongue, soldier of Captain George Mackay's Independent Company at Shiromore, 1746. [TGSI.LIII.370]

MACKAY, HUGH, in Oldshoremore, soldier of Captain George Mackay's Independent Company at Shiromore, dead by 1746. [TGSI.LIII.371]

MACKAY, HUGH, in Oldshorebeag, soldier of Captain George Mackay's Independent Company at Shiromore, dead by 1746. [TGSI.LIII.371]

MACKAY, HUGH, of Bighouse, Sutherland, 1752, 1770. [NAS.RD2.171/1.284; RD2.171/1.180; RD2.207.1072]

MACKAY, HUGH, a tenant farmer in Halladale, Caithness, 1756. [NAS.GD87.SEC2.13]

MACKAY, IUE, in Unapool, Assynt, Sutherland, 1774. [SA#88]

MCKAY, JAMES, in Skerray, 1740. [NAS.GD84/2/23]; probably Ensign of the Mackay Independent Company, 1745. [MCP.V.92]

MCKAY, JAMES, sergeant of Captain Hugh McKay's Independent Company in 1746. [TGSI.LIII.389]

MCKAY, JAMES, in Erriboll, a soldier of Captain Hugh McKay's Independent Company in 1746. [TGSI.LIII.391]

MACKAY, JAMES, in Torisdale, soldier of Captain George Mackay's Independent Company at Shiromore, 1746. [TGSI.LIII.371]

MACKAY, JAMES, in Hopes, soldier of Captain George Mackay's Independent Company at Shiromore, 1746. [TGSI.LIII.371]

MACKAY, Reverend JOHN, born 1680, minister at Durness, Sutherland, 1707-1714, then at Lairg, 1714-1753, died 23 February 1753, husband of Catherine Mackay who died in 1724. [Lairg gravestone, Sutherland][F.7.93]

MACKAY, JOHN, in Clunell, soldier of George Munro of Culcairns' Independent Company, 1745. [TGSI.LIII.364]

MACKAY, JOHN, born Talladale, 1656, "the blind piper", died 1754, father of Rorie. [Gairloch gravestone, Wester Ross]

MACKAY, JOHN, of Clashneach, 1737. [NAS.GD84/2/22, 23A]; probably a Lieutenant of the Mackay Independent Company, 1745. [MSP.V.92]

MACKAY, JOHN, of Mudale, Ensign of the Sutherland Company, 1745. [MCP.V.92]

MACKAY, JOHN, in Eribol, soldier of Captain George Mackay's Independent Company at Shiromore, 1746. [TGSI.LIII.371]

MACKAY, JOHN, in Kylestrome, soldier of Captain George Mackay's Independent Company at Shiromore, 1746. [TGSI.LIII.370]

MACKAY, JOHN, in Strathmore, soldier of Captain George Mackay's Independent Company at Shiromore, 1746. [TGSI.LIII.371]

MACKAY, JOHN, in Strathskerray, soldier of Captain George Mackay's Independent Company at Shiromore, 1746. [TGSI.LIII.370]

MCKAY, JOHN, in Melness, soldier of Captain Hugh McKay's Independent Company, discharged at Aviemore in 1746. [TGSI.LIII.390]

MCKAY, JOHN, in Cragan, a soldier of the Master of Ross' Independent Company at Linachan, 14 June 1746. [TGSI.LIII.391]

MCKAY, JOHN, in Melvich, soldier of Captain Hugh McKay's Independent Company, 17 June 1746. [TGSI.LIII.390]

MACKAY, JOHN, piper of Captain George Mackay's Independent Company at Shiromore, 1746. [TGSI.LIII.370]

MACKAY, JOHN, of Kirtomie, husband of Jean Mackay, disposition 1739. [NAS.GD87.Sec.2/8]

MCKAY, JOHN, in Sartigrim, soldier of Captain Hugh McKay's Independent Company, 17 June 1746. [TGSI.LIII.391]

MCKAY, JOHN, corporal of Alexander Gunn's Independent Company at Shiromore, 16 June 1746. [TGSI.LIII.369]

MCKAY, JOHN, in Rimusack, soldier of Alexander Gunn's Independent Company at Shiromore, 16 June 1746. [TGSI.LIII.369]

MCKAY, JOHN, in Mussoll, soldier of Captain Hugh McKay's Independent Company, 17 June 1746. [TGSI.LIII.391]

MCKAY, JOHN, in Evelacks, soldier of Alexander Gunn's Independent Company at Shiromore, 16 June 1746. [TGSI.LIII.369]

MCKAY, JOHN, in Kergarybeg, soldier of Captain Hugh McKay's Independent Company, 17 June 1746.
[TGSI.LIII.390]

MCKAY, JOHN, in Forsinard, soldier of Captain Hugh McKay's Independent Company, 17 June 1746.
[TGSI.LIII.390]

MCKAY, JOHN, a catechist, soldier of Captain Hugh McKay's Independent Company, 17 June 1746.
[TGSI.LIII.390]

MCKAY, JOHN, sergeant of Captain Hugh McKay's Independent Company in 1746. [TGSI.LIII.389]

MCKAY, JOHN, in Strathmelness, a soldier of Captain Hugh McKay's Independent Company in 1746.
[TGSI.LIII.390]

MCKAY, JOHN, in Clune, soldier of Alexander Gunn's Independent Company at Shiromore, 16 June 1746.
[TGSI.LIII.369]

MCKAY, JOHN, in Askaig, soldier of Alexander Gunn's Independent Company at Shiromore, 16 June 1746.
[TGSI.LIII.369]

MCKAY, JOHN, in Tongue, soldier of Captain Hugh McKay's Independent Company, 17 June 1746.
[TGSI.LIII.390]

MCKAY, JOHN BUY, soldier of Captain Alexander Mackenzie's Independent Company, 1746.
[TGSI.LIII.382]

MACKAY, Captain, JOHN, of Strathy, 1760.
[NAS.GD87.Sec.2/17]

MCKAY, JOHN, minister of Eddrachillis, Sutherland, from 1756 to 1762, then of Tongue, Sutherland, from 1762 to 1768, died 9 December 1768. Husband of Isobel Dewar.
[F.7.104, 110]

MACKAY, Lieutenant JOHN, of Oldany, tenant of Oldany and Lyne, Assynt, Sutherland, 1766, died by 1774, leaving Mrs Jean Mackay; Mrs Jean Mackay, four children and eight servants, in Oldany, Assynt, Sutherland, 1774. [SA#67/85]

MACKAY, JOHN, in Unapool, Assynt, Sutherland, 1774. [SA#88]

MCKAY, JOSEPH, in Nair, soldier of Captain Hugh McKay's Independent Company, discharged at Aviemore by Lord Loudoun, 1746. [TGSI.LIII.390]

MCKAY, MARGARET, born 1728, wife of John Sage a schoolmaster, died on 23 October 1769 in Kishorn. [Lochcarron gravestone]

MACKAY, MURDOCH, in Failliskard, soldier of Captain George Mackay's Independent Company at Shiromore, dead by 1746. [TGSI.LIII.370]

MACKAY, MURDOCH, in Scale, soldier of Captain George Mackay's Independent Company at Shiromore, 1746. [TGSI.LIII.371]

MACKAY, MURDOCH, in Eriboll, soldier of Captain George Mackay's Independent Company at Shiromore, 1746. [TGSI.LIII.371]

MCKAY, NEIL, in Niubeg, Durness, soldier of Captain Hugh McKay's Independent Company, 17 June 1746. [TGSI.LIII.391]

MACKAY, NEIL, in Borgie, soldier of Captain, George Mackay's Independent Company at Shiromore, 1746. [TGSI.LIII.370]

MACKAY, NEIL, a tenant in Halladale, Caithness, 1756. [NAS.GD87.SEC2.13]

MACKAY, NEIL, with his wife, and four children, in Culaig, Assynt, Sutherland, 1774. [SA#77]

MACKAY, ROBERT, in Clunnell, soldier of George Munro of Culcairns' Independent Company, 1745. [TGSI.LIII.364]

MCKAY, ROBERT, sergeant of Captain Hugh McKay's Independent Company in 1746. [TGSI.LIII.389]

MCKAY, ROBERT, in Torisdale, soldier of Captain Hugh McKay's Independent Company, 17 June 1746. [TGSI.LIII.390]

MACKAY, RODERICK, soldier of Captain George Mackay's Independent Company at Shiromore, 1746. [TGSI.LIII.371]

MCKAY, RODERICK, with his wife, and one servant, in Culin, Kirkton, Assynt, Sutherland, 1774. [SA#82]

MACKAY, THOMAS, born 2 August 1717, son of Reverend J. Mackay, died in 1803, minister at Lairg, Sutherland. Lairg gravestone, Sutherland][F.7.93]

MACKAY, WILLIAM, third son of Alexander Mackay. Minister of Tongue, Sutherland, from 1727 to 1728, died 21 October 1728. [F.7.109]

MACKAY, WILLIAM, of Pitfure, Lieutenant of the Sutherland Independent Company, in 1745.[MCP.V.92]

MACKAY, WILLIAM, in Pitfuir, soldier of George Munro of Culcairns' Independent Company, 1745. [TGSI.LIII.364]

MACKAY, WILLIAM, in Foulis, soldier of George Munro of Culcairns' Independent Company, 1745. [TGSI.LIII.364]

MCKAY, WILLIAM, in Knockdow, soldier of Captain Hugh McKay's Independent Company, 17 June 1746. [TGSI.LIII.391]

MACKAY, WILLIAM, in Mussol, soldier of Captain George Mackay's Independent Company at Shiromore, 1746. [TGSI.LIII.371]

MCKAY, WILLIAM, in Merikall, soldier of Alexander Gunn's Independent Company at Shiromore, 16 June 1746. [TGSI.LIII.369]

MACKAY, WILLIAM, in Ardvalin, soldier of Captain, George Mackay's Independent Company at Shiromore, dead by 1746. [TGSI.LIII.370]

MACKAY, WILLIAM, in Torrisdale, soldier of Captain, George Mackay's Independent Company at Shiromore, 1746. [TGSI.LIII.370]

MACKAY, WILLIAM, sergeant of Captain George Mackay's Independent Company at Shiromore, dead by 1746. [TGSI.LIII.370]

MCKAY, WILLIAM, in Ribigill, soldier of Captain Hugh McKay's Independent Company, 17 June 1746. [TGSI.LIII.390]

MACKAY, WILLIAM, in Ardbeag, soldier of Captain George Mackay's Independent Company at Shiromore, 1746. [TGSI.LIII.370]

MACKAY, WILLIAM, in Skerray, soldier of Captain George Mackay's Independent Company at Shiromore, dead by 1746. [TGSI.LIII.370]

MACKAY, WILLIAM, in Farr, Sutherland, soldier of Captain George Mackay's Independent Company at Shiromore, dead by 1746. [TGSI.LIII.371]

MACKAY, WILLIAM, a tenant in Halladale, Caithness, 1756. [NAS.GD87.SEC2.13]

MCKAY, WILLIAM, of Mellness, 1758. [NAS.GD84/2/47; GD87.Sec.2/15]

MCKAY, WILLIAM, with his wife, and child, in Culaig, Assynt, Sutherland, 1774. [SA#77]

MCKAY, WILLIAM, with his wife two children, and one servant, in Oldeny, Assynt, Sutherland, 1774. [SA#85]

MCKENLEY, ALEXANDER, a tenant in Tontlebegg, Halladale, Caithness, 1756. [NAS.GD87.SEC2.13]

MCKENUKRYZIE (?), JOSEPH, a tenant in Aucholdwullin, Halladale, Caithness, 1756. [NAS.GD87.SEC2.13]

MACKENZIE, ALEXANDER, Sergeant of Captain, Alexander Mackenzie's Independent Company, 1746. [TGSI.LIII.382]

MACKENZIE, ALEXANDER, in Achniselcih, soldier of Captain Alexander Mackenzie's Independent Company, 1746. [TGSI.LIII.382]

MACKENZIE, ALEXANDER, in Ballancra, soldier of Captain Alexander Mackenzie's Independent Company, deserted in 1746. [TGSI.LIII.382]

MACKENZIE, ALEXANDER, in Corlirie, soldier of Captain Alexander Mackenzie's Independent Company, 1746. [TGSI.LIII.382]

MACKENZIE, ALEXANDER, in Attadaile, soldier of Captain Alexander Mackenzie's Independent Company, 1746. [TGSI.LIII.382]

MACKENZIE, ALEXANDER, corporal of Captain Colin Mackenzie's Independent Company, 1746. [TGSI.LIII.384]

MACKENZIE, ALEXANDER, in Davoch, soldier of Captain Colin Mackenzie's Independent Company, 1746. [TGSI.LIII.384]

MCKENZIE, ALEXANDER, in Breakandond, soldier of Captain Colin Mackenzie's Independent Company, 1746. [TGSI.LIII.385]

MACKENZIE, ALEXANDER, in Achfary, soldier of Captain George Mackay's Independent Company at Shiromore, 1746. [TGSI.LIII.371]

MACKENZIE, ALEXANDER, in Borgie, soldier of Captain, George Mackay's Independent Company at Shiromore, 1746. [TGSI.LIII.371]

MCKENZIE, ALEXANDER, of Davachmalnach, 1752. [NAS.RD4.178/1.594]

MCKENZIE, ALEXANDER, was served as heir to his great grandfather Alexander McKenzie of Ballon, parish of Loch Broom, Wester Ross, who died in 1714, on 2 September 1756. [NAS.SH]

MCKENZIE, ALEXANDER, of Fairburn, tacksman of the salmon fishings on the Water of Conan, and his son Roderick McKenzie of Fairburn, 1756 to 1770. [NAS.E746.125]

MCKENZIE, ALEXANDER, of Inchcoulter, 1766. [NAS.E746.10]

MCKENZIE, ALEXANDER, of Ardloch, tenant farmer, Culag, and Filin, Assynt, Sutherland, 1766 and 1775. [SA#67]

MCKENZIE, ALEXANDER, sr., a silversmith in Tain, Easter Ross, 1766. [OR#408]

MCKENZIE, ALEXANDER, jr., a silversmith in Tain, Easter Ross, 1766. [OR#408]

MCKENZIE, ALEXANDER, tenant in Dornie, 1770. [NAS.E746.167.4]

MCKENZIE, ALEXANDER, tacksman of Dingwall, Ross and Cromarty, 1773. [NAS.GD46.SEC.1/212]

MCKENZIE, ALEXANDER, with his wife and two children, in Ardvar, Assynt, Sutherland, 1774. [SA#72]

MCKENZIE, ALEXANDER, in Badigrinan, Assynt, Sutherland, 1774. [SA#73]

MCKENZIE, ALEXANDER, wife, and father, in Badidarroch, Assynt, Sutherland, 1774. [SA#73]

MCKENZIE, ALEXANDER, tenant farmer, Eadar a Chalda, Assynt, Sutherland, 1775. [SA#67]

MCKENZIE, ALEXANDER, wife, two children, and a servant, in Badidarroch, Assynt, Sutherland, 1774. [SA#73]

MACKENZIE, ALEXANDER, in Drumswordland, Assynt, Sutherland, 1774. [SA#79]

MCKENZIE, ALEXANDER, with his wife, and two children, in Clachtole, Assynt, Sutherland, 1774. [SA#74]

MACKENZIE, ALEXANDER, with his wife, and three children, in Clasnhessie, Assynt, Sutherland, 1774. [SA#76]

MCKENZIE, ALEXANDER, a pedlar, in Culaig, Assynt, Sutherland, 1774. [SA#77]

MCKENZIE, ALEXANDER, with his wife, four children, and three servants in Edrachalda, Assynt, Sutherland, 1774. [SA#80]

MCKENZIE, ALEXANDER, of Ardloch, in Fillin, Assynt, Sutherland, 1774. [SA#80]

MCKENZIE, ALEXANDER, with his mother, and two children, in Glonlcrag, Assynt, Sutherland, 1774. [SA#80]

MCKENZIE, ALEXANDER, of Ardloch, with his wife, in Leadbeg, Assynt, Sutherland, 1774. [SA#83]

MCKENZIE, ALEXANDER, with his wife, one child and one servant, in Stronchrubie, Assynt, Sutherland, 1774. [SA#87]

MCKENZIE, ANGUS, with his wife, and one servant, in Stronchrubie, Assynt, Sutherland, 1774. [SA#87]

MACKENZIE, ANNABEL, a widow, with two children, and two servants, in Culkin Drumbeg, Assynt, Sutherland, 1774. [SA#78]

MCKENZIE, BARBARA, a widow with four children, in Unapool, Assynt, Sutherland, 1774. [SA#88]

MACKENZIE, CHRISTIAN, in Culkin Drumbeg, Assynt, Sutherland, 1774. [SA#79]

MCKENZIE, CHRISTOPHER, tenant in Dalkinloch, 1770. [NAS.E746.167.5]

MACKENZIE, COLIN, in Cullnokill, Applecross, Wester Ross,, 1718. [TGSI.LIV.452]

MACKENZIE, COLIN, of Glack, born 1707 son of Roderick Mackenzie of Brae and Longcroft, educated at King's College, Aberdeen, minister of Fodderty, Kinettas, and Glen Ussie from 1735 to 1778, chaplain to the 73rd Regiment (Macleod's Highlanders) 1778, died 8 March 1801. Husband of (1) Margaret Rose, parents of Margaret; (2) Mary Mackenzie, parents of Anne, Una, Isabel, Roderick, Johanna, Mary, John, Beatrice, Donald, Forbes, and Jean. [F.7.37]

MCKENZIE, COLIN, Captain of the Seaforth Independent Company at Inverness, 1745. '[MCP.V.92]

MACKENZIE, COLIN, in Dingwall, Ross and Cromarty, 29 January 1751. [NAS.RD3.211.103]

MACKENZIE, COLIN, a baillie in Dingwall, Ross and Cromarty, 1766. [NAS.E746.96]

MACKENZIE, COLIN, a kelp merchant at Lochbroom, Wester Ross, 1770. [NAS.E746.125]

MCKENZIE, COLIN, in Reanchine, 1773. [NAS.E746.79]

MACKENZIE, COLIN, with his two sisters, in Clasnhessie, Assynt, Sutherland, 1774. [SA#76]

MCKENZIE, COLIN, with his wife, one child, and one servant, in Glenlerag, Assynt, Sutherland, 1774. [SA#80]

MCKENZIE, DANIEL, at Blackhill, 1780.NAS.E746.81]

MCKENZIE, DANIEL, tenant in the barony of New Tarbat, Easter Ross, 1767 to 1774. [NAS.E746.92]

MCKENZIE, DANIEL, in Achiltibuie, Sutherland, 1771. [NAS.E746.79]

MCKENZIE, DONALD, a corporal in Captain Hugh McLeod of Geanies Independent Company on 17 June 1746. [TGSI.LIII.380]

MACKENZIE, DONALD, in Strome, soldier of Captain Alexander Mackenzie's Independent Company, 1746. [TGSI.LIII.382]

MACKENZIE, DONALD, in Castlestrom, soldier of Captain, Alexander Mackenzie's Independent Company, 1746. [TGSI.LIII.382]

MACKENZIE, DONALD, in Davoch, soldier of Captain Colin Mackenzie's Independent Company, 1746. [TGSI.LIII.384]

MACKENZIE, DONALD, with his wife and five children, in Balchladich, Assynt, Sutherland, 1774. [SA#74]

MCKENZIE, DONALD, with his wife, and five children, in Glenlerag, Assynt, Sutherland, 1774. [SA#80]

MACKENZIE, DONALD, with his wife, and five children, in Clasnhessie, Assynt, Sutherland, 1774. [SA#76]

MCKENZIE, DONALD, with his wife, and two children, in Clasnhessie, Assynt, Sutherland, 1774. [SA#76]

MCKENZIE, DONALD, with his wife, and one servant, in Culkin Drumbeg, Assynt, Sutherland, 1774. [SA#78]

MCKENZIE, DONALD, with his wife, and two children, in Culin, Kirkton, Assynt, Sutherland, 1774. [SA#82]

MCKENZIE, or MCKUNCY, DONALD, with his wife, one child, and one servant, in Glenlerag, Assynt, Sutherland, 1774. [SA#80]

MACKENZIE, DONALD, in Ledmore, Assynt, Sutherland, 1774. [SA#84]

MCKENZIE, DONALD, the elder, in Nedd, Assynt, Sutherland, 1774. [SA#85]

MCKENZIE, DONALD, with his wife, and two servants, in Rhintraid, Assynt, Sutherland, 1774. [SA#86]

MCKENZIE, DONALD in Unapool, Assynt, Sutherland, 1774. [SA#88]

MACKENZIE, DONALD, in Midstrom, soldier of Captain Alexander Mackenzie's Independent Company, dead by 1746. [TGSI.LIII.382]

MACKENZIE, DUNCAN, in Midstrom, soldier of Captain Alexander Mackenzie's Independent Company, dead by 1746. [TGSI.LIII.382]

MACKENZIE, DUNCAN, tacksman of Dingwall, Ross and Cromarty, 1767-1773. [NAS.GD46.SEC.1/212]

MACKENZIE, FARQUHAR, in Achnishin, soldier of Captain Alexander Mackenzie's Independent Company, 1746. [TGSI.LIII.382]

MACKENZIE, FARQUHAR, in Attadaile, soldier of Captain Alexander Mackenzie's Independent Company, 1746. [TGSI.LIII.382]

MCKENZIE, GEORGE, in Culcairn, a soldier in Captain Hugh McLeod of Geanies Independent Company on 17 June 1746. [TGSI.LIII.381]

MCKENZIE, GEORGE, in Kirkiboll, soldier of Captain Hugh McKay's Independent Company, 17 June 1746. [TGSI.LIII.390]

MCKENZIE, GEORGE, tenant in Achnahaird, 1756. [NAS.E746.97/113.5]

MCKENZIE, GEORGE, at Apituild, 1780. [NAS.E746.81]

MCKENZIE, GEORGE, at Middal, 1780. [NAS.E746.81]

MCKENZIE, GUSTAVUS, a merchant in Tain, Easter Ross, 1766. [OR#408]

MCKENZIE, HECTOR, born 1700 son of Charles McKenzie of Letterewe, educated at King's College, Aberdeen, college librarian 1721, assistant schoolmaster, minister of Fodderty, Kinettas, and Glen Ussie from 1727 to 1734, died 27 February 1734. Husband of Jean Baillie. [F.7.37]

MCKENZIE, HECTOR, a soldier of Captain Hugh McKay's Independent Company in 1746. [TGSI.LIII.390]

MCKENZIE, HECTOR, in Knockbean, soldier of Captain Colin Mackenzie's Independent Company, 1746. [TGSI.LIII.384]

MCKENZIE, HECTOR, a catechist, with his wife, and four children, in Clashmore, Assynt, Sutherland, 1774. [SA#75]

MCKENZIE, HECTOR, with his wife, five children, and two servants, in Unapool, Assynt, Sutherland, 1774. [SA#88]

MACKENZIE, HECTOR, factor for the barony of Coigach, 1774. [NAS.E746.76]

MCKENZIE, HENRY, with his wife, and three children, in Clashmore, Assynt, Sutherland, 1774. [SA#75]

MCKENZIE, HUGH, soldier of Captain Hugh McKay's Independent Company, 17 June 1746. [TGSI.LIII.391]

MCKENZIE, JAMES, born 1703, tacksman, sometime in Bracklach, Lochcarron, died 13 November 1761. [Lochcarron gravestone]

MCKENZIE, JOHN, in Blaud, Applecross, Wester Ross, 1718. [TGSI.LIV.450]

MCKENZIE, JOHN, in Kirkton of Applecross, Wester Ross,, 1718. [TGSI.LIV.451]

MCKENZIE, JOHN, in Portchamile, soldier of Captain Hugh McKay's Independent Company, 17 June 1746. [TGSI.LIII.390]

MACKENZIE, JOHN, sr., Sergeant of Captain Alexander Mackenzie's Independent Company, 1746. [TGSI.LIII.382]

MACKENZIE, JOHN, jr., Sergeant of Captain Alexander Mackenzie's Independent Company, deserted in 1746. [TGSI.LIII.382]

MCKENZIE, JOHN, in Achniselich, soldier of Captain Alexander Mackenzie's Independent Company, 1746. [TGSI.LIII.382]

MACKENZIE, JOHN, in Salchy, soldier of Captain Alexander Mackenzie's Independent Company, dead by 1746. [TGSI.LIII.382]

MACKENZIE, JOHN BAIN, soldier of Captain Alexander Mackenzie's Independent Company, 1746. [TGSI.LIII.382]

MCKENZIE, JOHN, in Knockbean, soldier of Captain Colin Mackenzie's Independent Company, 1746. [TGSI.LIII.384]

MACKENZIE, JOHN, soldier of Captain George Mackay's Independent Company at Shiromore, 1746. [TGSI.LIII.371]

MACKENZIE, JOHN, tacksman of Dingwall, Ross and Cromarty, 1767. [NAS.GD46.SEC.1/212]

MCKENZIE, JOHN, of Applecross, Wester Ross, 1747, 1770. [NAS.RD4.178/1.539; RD2.207.949; E746.99/146]

MCKENZIE, JOHN, at Lochbroom, Wester Ross, 1770. [NAS.RD2.208.252]

MCKENZIE, JOHN, tenant in Dalkinloch, 1770. [NAS.E746.167.5]

MCKENZIE, JOHN, with his wife, three children, and two servants, in Ardvar, Assynt, Sutherland, 1774. [SA#72]

MCKENZIE, JOHN, with his wife, and four children, in Clachtole, Assynt, Sutherland, 1774. [SA#74]

MCKENZIE, JOHN, John McKenzie Hector's son, with his wife, and three servants, in Clashmore, Assynt, Sutherland, 1774. [SA#75]

MACKENZIE, JOHN, with his wife, one child and one servant, in Culkin Drumbeg, Assynt, Sutherland, 1774. [SA#78]

MCKENZIE, JOHN, with his wife, and two children, in Glenlerag, Assynt, Sutherland, 1774. [SA#80]

MACKENZIE, JOHN, in Culkein Achnacarnan, Assynt, Sutherland, 1774. [SA#78]

MCKENZIE, JOHN, with his wife, child, and one servant, in Clashmore, Assynt, Sutherland, 1774. [SA#75]

MCKENZIE, JOHN, with his wife, and three children in Elphine, Assynt, Sutherland, 1774. [SA#80]

MACKENZIE, JOHN, with his wife, one child, and one servant, in Riancrevich, Ledmore, Assynt, Sutherland, 1774. [SA#84]

MCKENZIE, or MCALISTER, JOHN, with his wife, two children, and one servant, in Knocknach, Assynt, Sutherland, 1774. [SA#76]

MCKENZIE, JOHN, with his wife and six children, in Nedd, Assynt, Sutherland, 1774. [SA#85]

MCKENZIE, JOHN, with his wife, three children and one servant, in Rhintraid, Assynt, Sutherland, 1774. [SA#86]

MCKENZIE, JOHN, in Unapool, Assynt, Sutherland, 1774. [SA#88]

MCKENZIE, JOHN, tacksman of Kenachrine, Coigach, 1782. [NAS.E746.79]

MCKENZIE, KATHARINE, a widow, with three children, in Clachtole, Assynt, Sutherland, 1774. [SA#74]

MCKENZIE, KATHRINE, with her, two children, in Clasnhessie, Assynt, Sutherland, 1774. [SA#76]

MCKENZIE, KENNETH, in Kirkton of Applecross, Wester Ross,, 1718. [TGSI.LIV.451]

MACKENZIE, KENNETH, sergeant of Captain Colin Mackenzie's Independent Company, 1746. [TGSI.LIII.384]

MCKENZIE, KENNETH, in Achiness, soldier of Captain Colin Mackenzie's Independent Company, 1746. [TGSI.LIII.384]

MCKENZIE, KENNETH, of Dundonnel, 1752, 1768. [NAS.RD4.178/1.234; E746.97]

MACKENZIE, or MACEANOIG, KENNETH, tacksman of Urray, 1767, and his wife Margaret MacLennan. [NAS.GD46.SEC.1/212]

MCKENZIE, KENNETH, of Inchnadamph, tenant farmer, Baddirach, Tubeg, and of Cnoc nan Each, Assynt, Sutherland, 1766 and 1775. [SA#66]

MCKENZIE, KENNETH, with his wife, and six servants in Elphine, Assynt, Sutherland, 1774. [SA#80]

MCKENZIE, KENNETH, in Inverkirkaig, Badinamban, Assynt, Sutherland, 1774. [SA#74]

MCKENZIE, KENNETH, tenant farmer, Inverkirkaig, Assynt, Sutherland, 1766 and 1775. [SA#67]

MCKENZIE, KENNETH, with his wife, two children, and two servants in Culaig, Assynt, Sutherland, 1774. [SA#77]

MCKENZIE, KENNETH, with his wife, and six children, in Clasnhessie, Assynt, Sutherland, 1774. [SA#76]

MCKENZIE, KENNETH, with three children, in Achnacarnan, Assynt, Sutherland, 1774. [SA#72]

MCKENZIE, KENNETH, with his wife, four children, and five servants, in Inchnadamff, Assynt, Sutherland, 1774. [SA#80]

MCKENZIE, KENNETH, with his wife, four children, and five servants, in Inverkirkaig, Assynt, Sutherland, 1774. [SA#80]

MCKENZIE, KENNETH, a tailor, with his wife, one child and one servant, in Knockan, Assynt, Sutherland, 1774. [SA#82]

MCKENZIE, or MCALLISTER, KENNETH ROY, with his wife, and five children, in Clashmore, Assynt, Sutherland, 1774. [SA#75]

MCKENZIE, or MCACHAN, KENNETH, with his wife, and three children, in Clashmore, Assynt, Sutherland, 1774. [SA#75]

MCKENZIE, KENNETH, with his wife and four children, in Nedd, Assynt, Sutherland, 1774. [SA#85]

MCKENZIE, KENNETH, in Inchnadamff, and Upper Tubeg, Assynt, Sutherland, 1774. [SA#87]

MCKENZIE, LACHLAN, with his wife, eight children, and a servant, in Clachtole, Assynt, Sutherland, 1774. [SA#74]

MCKENZIE, MARY, a widow with four children, in Nedd, Assynt, Sutherland, 1774. [SA#85]

MCKENZIE, MURDO, the younger of Ardross, 1752. [NAS.RD3.211/2.450]

MCKENZIE, MURDO, tenant of the farm of Corry and Dalvraid in 1757, baron baillie of Coigach, 1760. [NAS.E746.113.20]

MCKENZIE, MURDO, with his wife and child, in Ardvar, Assynt, Sutherland, 1774. [SA#73]

MCKENZIE, MURDO, with his wife, and two servants, in Drumbeg, Assynt, Sutherland, 1774. [SA#79]

MCKENZIE, MURDO, with his wife, two children, and two servants, in Glenlerag, Assynt, Sutherland, 1774. [SA#80]

MACKENZIE, MURDO, with his wife, three children and four servants, in Stronchrubie, Assynt, Sutherland, 1774. [SA#86]

MCKENZIE, MURDO, in Stronchrubie, and Tubeg, Assynt, Sutherland, 1774. [SA#87]

MCKENZIE, MURDO MACALISTER, in Tubeg, Assynt, Sutherland, 1774. [SA#87]

MCKENZIE, MURDO, with his wife, and three children, in Unapool, Assynt, Sutherland, 1774. [SA#88]

MCKENZIE, MURDO, a widower, with six children, in Achnacarnan, Assynt, Sutherland, 1774. [SA#72]

MCKENZIE, MURDO, in Clachtole, Assynt, Sutherland, 1774. [SA#74]

MCKENZIE, MURDOCH, in Tronimbrass, Applecross, Wester Ross, 1718. [TGSI.LIV.450]

MCKENZIE, MURDOCH, minister of Contin and Strathgarve from 1732 to 1741. [F.7.31]

MCKENZIE, MURDOCH, in Main, soldier of Captain Colin Mackenzie's Independent Company, 1746. [TGSI.LIII.384]

MCKENZIE, MURDOCH, in Drumanbuy, soldier of Captain Colin Mackenzie's Independent Company, 1746. [TGSI.LIII.385]

MCKENZIE, MURDOCH, of Achilty, 1757. [NAS.E746.113.11]

MCKENZIE, MURDOCH, of Stronechrubie, tenant farmer, Stronechrubie, 1766. [SA#67]

MCKENZIE, MURDOCH, wife, three children, and two servants, in Badigrinan, Assynt, Sutherland, 1774. [SA#73]

MCKENZIE, MURDOCH, with his wife and three children, in Culin, Kirkton, Assynt, Sutherland, 1774. [SA#82]

MACKENZIE, or MCALLISTER, MURDOCH, with his wife, and one servant, in Culkin Drumbeg, Assynt, Sutherland, 1774. [SA#78]

MACKENZIE, NIEL, tacksman of Fodderty, Easter Ross, 1773. [NAS.GD46.SEC.1/212]

MACKENZIE, RODERICK, corporal of Captain Alexander Mackenzie's Independent Company, 1746. [TGSI.LIII.382]

MCKENZIE, RODERICK, of Redcastle, the Black Isle, 1751. [NAS.RD4.178/2.430]

MCKENZIE, RODERICK, in Rive, 1765.
[NAS.E746.113.1/2]

MCKENZIE, RODERICK, with his wife, and two children, in Ardvar, Assynt, Sutherland, 1774. [SA#73]

MCKENZIE, RODERICK, miller, with his wife, two children, and four servants, in Glenlerag, Assynt, Sutherland, 1774. [SA#80]

MCKENZIE, RODERICK, with his wife, two children, and two servants in Elphine, Assynt, Sutherland, 1774. [SA#80]

MCKENZIE, RODERICK, in Layne, Assynt, Sutherland, 1774. [SA#85]

MCKENZIE, RORY, with his wife, and three children, in Culkein Achnacarnan, Assynt, Sutherland, 1774. [SA#78]

MCKENZIE, SIMON, in Langwall, 1764. [NAS.E746.79]

MCKENZIE, THOMAS, born 1702, a tenant farmer in Balmaclach, died on 3 February 1762. [Golspie gravestone, Sutherland]

MCKENZIE, WILLIAM, in Glen, Applecross, Wester Ross, 1718. [TGSI.LIV.451]

MCKENZIE, WILLIAM, in Lochcarron, soldier of Captain Alexander Mackenzie's Independent Company, 1746. [TGSI.LIII.382]

MACKENZIE, WILLIAM, in Golspie, Sutherland, soldier of Captain George Mackay's Independent Company at Shiromore, 1746. [TGSI.LIII.371]

MACKENZIE, WILLIAM, in Rians, soldier of Captain George Mackay's Independent Company at Shiromore, dead by 1746. [TGSI.LIII.371]

MCKENZIE, WILLIAM, in Lochalsh, soldier of Captain Alexander Mackenzie's Independent Company, 1746. [TGSI.LIII.382]

MCKENZIE, WILLIAM, minister of Assynt, Sutherland, with his wife, three children, and eight servants, in Cullin and Camore, Kirkton, and in Torbreck, 1766, 1775. [SA#67/82/87]; born 1734, graduated MA from Marischal College, Aberdeen, 1755, schoolmaster in Stornaway, ordained to Harris in 1762, minister of Assynt from 1765 to 1812, died 27 November 1816. Married Margaret, daughter of Reverend Patrick Grant, 19 June 1765. Parents of Wilhelmina Maxwell born 1766, Anna born 1768, died 1769, John born 1769, died 1770, Patrick born 1771, died 1799, Robson born 1773, John born 1775, died 1778, Alexander born 1778, twin Jean Young born 1778, Elizabeth born 1782, died 1806, Colin born 1783, died 1805, and Joseph born 1785. [F.7.78]

MCKENZIE, WILLIAM, born 1738 son of John McKenzie, farmer at Kilmuir Easter, Ross and Cromarty, and Grace Crombie, minister of Tongue, Sutherland, from 1769. Husband of Jean Porteous, and father of Grizel, Hugh, William, Helen, Anne, John (a surgeon in Jamaica), and Jean. Died 5 January 1834. [F.7.110]

MCKENZIE, WILLIAM, with his wife, child, and one servant, in Clashmore, Assynt, Sutherland, 1774. [SA#75]

MCKENZIE, WILLIAM, with his wife, three children and two servants, in Clasnhessie, Assynt, Sutherland, 1774. [SA#76]

MCKENZIE, WILLIAM, with his wife, and four servants in Elphine, Assynt, Sutherland, 1774. [SA#80]

MCKENZIE, WILLIAM, with his wife, and one servant, in Culin, Kirkton, Assynt, Sutherland, 1774. [SA#82]

MCKENZIE, or MCRORY, WILLIAM, with his wife, and two children, in Clachtole, Assynt, Sutherland, 1774. [SA#74]

MCKENZIE, WILLIAM, a widower with two children, and four servants, in Layne, Assynt, Sutherland, 1774. [SA#84]

MCKINLAY, ALEXANDER, a tenant in Halladale, Caithness, 1756. [NAS.GD87.SEC2.13]

MCKINTOSH, JOHN, with his wife, and three children, in Stronchrubie, Assynt, Sutherland, 1774. [SA#87]

MCKOL VICHOMASH, ALEXANDER, with his wife, three children and servants, in Oldany, Assynt, Sutherland, 1774. [SA#85]

MCKOLVAN or MCONEILVAIN, ALEXANDER MCLEOD, with his wife and four children in Achmelvich, Assynt, Sutherland, 1774. [SA#71]

MCKY, WILLIAM, in Breckrue, a soldier of Captain Hugh McKay's Independent Company in 1746. [TGSI.LIII.391]

MCLACH, WILLIAM ROSS, in Langland, a soldier of the Master of Ross' Independent Company at Linachan, 14 June 1746. [TGSI.LIII.391]

MCLACHLAN, DONALD, in Glenlerag, Assynt, Sutherland, 1774. [SA#80]

MCLEA, FINLAY, in Strathconnon, soldier of Captain Colin Mackenzie's Independent Company, 1746. [TGSI.LIII.385]

MCLEAN, ALEXANDER, with his wife, two children, and one servant, in Glenlerag, Assynt, Sutherland, 1774. [SA#80]

MCLEAN, or MACALISTER, ALEXANDER, with his wife, and three children, in Glenlerag, Assynt, Sutherland, 1774. [SA#80]

MCLEAN, BARBARA, a widow, in Inverkirkaig, Assynt, Sutherland, 1774. [SA#82]

MCLEAN, DAVID, in Altas, a soldier in Captain Hugh McLeod of Geanies Independent Company on 17 June 1746. [TGSI.LIII.381]

MCLEAN, DONALD, in Achniselich, soldier of Captain Alexander Mackenzie's Independent Company, 1746. [TGSI.LIII.382]

MACLEAN, DONALD, soldier of Captain George Mackay's Independent Company at Shiromore, 1746. [TGSI.LIII.371]

MCLEAN, DONALD, with his wife and two servants, in Nedd, Assynt, Sutherland, 1774. [SA#85]

MACLEAN, DUNCAN, in Milntown, soldier of George Munro of Culcairns' Independent Company, 1745. [TGSI.LIII.364]

MACLEAN, DUNCAN, in Attadaile, soldier of Captain Alexander Mackenzie's Independent Company, 1746. [TGSI.LIII.383]

MCLEAN, DUNCAN, tenant in Dornie, 1770. [NAS.E746.167.4]

MCLEAN, GUSTAVUS, a soldier in Captain Hugh McLeod of Geanies Independent Company on 17 June 1746. [TGSI.LIII.380]

MCLEAN, JOHN, a soldier of the Master of Ross' Independent Company at Linachan, 14 June 1746. [TGSI.LIII.391]

MCLEAN, JOHN, in Inverkirkaig, Assynt, Sutherland, 1774. [SA#82]

MCLEAN, JOHN, with his wife and one servant, in Unapool, Assynt, Sutherland, 1774. [SA#88]

MCLEAN, KENNETH, with his wife, two children, and one servant, in Inver, Assynt, Sutherland, 1774. [SA#80]

MCLEAN, KENNETH, with his wife, and two servants, in Glaskoil, Leadmore, Assynt, Sutherland, 1774. [SA#83]

MCLEAN, or BAYNE, KENNETH, with his wife, two children and one servant, in Inverkirkaig, Assynt, Sutherland, 1774. [SA#82]

MCLEAN, MARY, a widow, with five children, in Achnacarnan, Assynt, Sutherland, 1774. [SA#72]

MCLEAN, NEIL, in Altas, a soldier in Captain Hugh McLeod of Geanies Independent Company on 17 June 1746. [TGSI.LIII.380]

MACLEAN, WILLIAM, in Dibidill, soldier of George Munro of Culcairns' Independent Company, 1745. [TGSI.LIII.364]

MCLEAN, WILLIAM, with his wife, and three children, in Ardvar, Assynt, Sutherland, 1774. [SA#73]

MCLEAN, ..., a widow, in Knockan, Assynt, Sutherland, 1774. [SA#83]

MACLENNAN, ALEXANDER, in Morvich, soldier of Captain Colin Mackenzie's Independent Company, 1746. [TGSI.LIII.384]

MACLENNAN, ALEXANDER, in Little Oassie, soldier of Captain Colin Mackenzie's Independent Company, 1746. [TGSI.LIII.385]

MACLENNAN, ALEXANDER, tacksman of Fodderty, 1776. [NAS.GD46.SEC.1/212]

MACLENNAN, ANDREW, in Tain, Easter Ross, 1766.
[OR#409]

MACLENNAN, DONALD, corporal of Captain Alexander
Mackenzie's Independent Company, 1746.
[TGSI.LIII.382]

MCLENNAN, DONALD, in Kirkton, soldier of Captain
Alexander Mackenzie's Independent Company, 1746.
[TGSI.LIII.383]

MACLENNAN, DONALD, in Corvike, soldier of Captain
Colin Mackenzie's Independent Company, 1746.
[TGSI.LIII.384]

MACLENNAN, DONALD, a shoemaker in Tain, Easter Ross,
1766. [OR#409]

MCLENNAN, DONALD, tenant in Dalkinloch, 1770.
[NAS.E746.167.5]

MCLENNAN, DONALD, born 1716, smith at Lochcarron,
Wester Ross, died in June 1777, husband of Katherine.
[Lochcarron gravestone]

MACLENNAN, GEORGE, in Brahan, soldier of Captain
Alexander Mackenzie's Independent Company, 1746.
[TGSI.LIII.382]

MACLENNAN, GEORGE, tacksman of Urray, Ross and
Cromarty, 1767-1773. [NAS.GD46.SEC.1/212]

MCLENNAN, JOHN, in Achiglee, soldier of Captain
Alexander Mackenzie's Independent Company, 1746.
[TGSI.LIII.382]

MCLENNAN, JOHN, in Belblear, soldier of Captain Colin
Mackenzie's Independent Company, 1746.
[TGSI.LIII.385]

MCLENNAN, JOHN, tacksman of Fodderty, Ross and
Cromarty, 1767-1773. [NAS.GD46.SEC.1/212]

MCLENNAN, JOHN, educated at St Andrews, minister of Contin and Strathgarve, Ross and Cromarty, from 1742 to 1775, died 28 April 1775. Husband of Helen Grant, parents of John, Alexander, Janet, Margaret, Louis, George, Isabel, Elizabeth, John, and James. [F.7.31]

MACLENNAN, KENNETH, in Lichican, soldier of Captain Colin Mackenzie's Independent Company, 1746. [TGSI.LIII.384]

MACLENNAN, KENNETH, in Cainloch, soldier of Captain Colin Mackenzie's Independent Company, 1746. [TGSI.LIII.385]

MCLENNAN, KENNETH, tacksman of Fodderty, 1766-1773. [NAS.GD46.SEC.1/212]

MCLENNAN, MURDO, tacksman of Urray, Ross and Cromarty, 1767. [NAS.GD46.SEC.1/212]

MACLENNAN, MURDOCH, in Achyark, soldier of Captain Colin Mackenzie's Independent Company, 1746. [TGSI.LIII.384]

MACLENNAN, RODERICK, tacksman of Dingwall, Ross and Cromarty, 1767-1773. [NAS.GD46.SEC.1/212]

MCLEOD, AENEAS, tacksman of Shiniscaig and Lochanganvich, from 1740. [NAS.E746.113.23/1]

MCLEOD, ALEXANDER, in Drumsordlan, a soldier in Captain Hugh McLeod of Geanies Independent Company on 17 June 1746. [TGSI.LIII.380]

MCLEOD, ALEXANDER, in Store, a soldier in Captain Hugh McLeod of Geanies Independent Company on 17 June 1746. [TGSI.LIII.380]

MCLEOD, ALEXANDER, in Knokneach, a soldier in Captain Hugh McLeod of Geanies Independent Company on 17 June 1746. [TGSI.LIII.380]

MCLEOD, ALEXANDER, in Ledmore, a soldier in Captain Hugh McLeod of Geanies Independent Company on 17 June 1746. [TGSI.LIII.380]

MCLEOD, ALEXANDER, in Turnack, a soldier of the Master of Ross' Independent Company at Linachan, 14 June 1746. [TGSI.LIII.392]

MCLEOD, ALEXANDER, in Culknie, a soldier in Captain Hugh McLeod of Geanies Independent Company on 17 June 1746. [TGSI.LIII.380]

MCLEOD, ALEXANDER, in Turnack, a soldier of the Master of Ross' Independent Company at Linachan, 14 June 1746. [TGSI.LIII.392]

MCLEOD, ALEXANDER, a merchant in Inverness, 1752. [NAS.RD3.211/2.125]

MCLEOD, Lieutenant ALEXANDER, of Ledmore, tenant farmer, Aultnachie, Ledmore and Bad a Ghrianan, Assynt, Sutherland, 1766, 1775. [SA#66]

MCLEOD, ALEXANDER, tenant in Dalkinloch, 1770. [NAS.E746.167.5]

MCLEOD, ALEXANDER, wife, child, and two servants, in Auldnachy, Assynt, Sutherland, 1774. [SA#73]

MCLEOD, ALEXANDER, in Culaig, Assynt, Sutherland, 1774. [SA#77]

MCLEOD, ALEXANDER, with his wife and servant, in Balchladich, Assynt, Sutherland, 1774. [SA#74]

MCLEOD, ALEXANDER, with his wife, five children, and a servant, in Brakloch, Assynt, Sutherland, 1774. [SA#74]

MCLEOD, ALEXANDER, with his wife, three children, and one servant, in Inchnadamff, Assynt, Sutherland, 1774. [SA#80]

MCLEOD, or MCNEIL, ALEXANDER, wife, and five children, in Badidarroch, Assynt, Sutherland, 1774. [SA#73]

MCLEOD, ALEXANDER, wife, and servant, in Badidarroch, Assynt, Sutherland, 1774. [SA#73]

MCLEOD, ALEXANDER, son in law of Donald McLeod McInnash, with his wife, in Clasnhessie, Assynt, Sutherland, 1774. [SA#76]

MCLEOD, or MCRORY, ALEXANDER, in Badidarroch, Assynt, Sutherland, 1774. [SA#73]

MACLEOD, ALEXANDER, with his wife, one child, and one servant, in Duchlash, Assynt, Sutherland, 1774. [SA#79]

MCLEOD, ALEXANDER, with his wife, and two children, in Ledmore, Assynt, Sutherland, 1774. [SA#84]

MACLEOD, ALEXANDER, with his wife, and four children, in Stoer, Assynt, Sutherland, 1774. [SA#86]

MCLEOD, ALEXANDER, with his wife, and five children, in Layne, Assynt, Sutherland, 1774. [SA#85]

MCLEOD, ANGUS, in Frie, soldier of Alexander Gunn's Independent Company at Shiromore, 16 June 1746. [TGSI.LIII.369]

MCLEOD, ANGUS, in Durness, Sutherland, soldier of Captain Hugh McKay's Independent Company, 17 June 1746. [TGSI.LIII.390]

MCLEOD, ANGUS, in Knockneach, a soldier in Captain Hugh McLeod of Geanies Independent Company on 17 June 1746. [TGSI.LIII.380]

MCLEOD, ANGUS, in Stroncruby, a soldier in Captain Hugh McLeod of Geanies Independent Company on 17 June 1746. [TGSI.LIII.380]

MCLEOD, ANGUS, sr., in Ledmore, a soldier in Captain
Hugh McLeod of Geanies' Independent Company on 17
June 1746. [TGSI.LIII.380]

MCLEOD, ANGUS, jr., in Ledmore, a soldier in Captain
Hugh McLeod of Geanies Independent Company on 17
June 1746. [TGSI.LIII.380]

MCLEOD, ANGUS, in Inchnadamph, a soldier in Captain
Hugh McLeod of Geanies' Independent Company on 17
June 1746. [TGSI.LIII.380]

MCLEOD, ANGUS, in Inver, a soldier in Captain Hugh
McLeod of Geanies' Independent Company on 17 June
1746. [TGSI.LIII.380]

MCLEOD, ANGUS, in Hope, soldier of Captain Hugh
McKay's Independent Company, 17 June 1746.
[TGSI.LIII.390]

MCLEOD, ANGUS, in Achmelvich, a soldier in Captain
Hugh McLeod of Geanies' Independent Company on 17
June 1746. [TGSI.LIII.380]

MCLEOD, ANGUS, soldier of Captain George Mackay's
Independent Company at Shiromore, 1746.
[TGSI.LIII.371]

MCLEOD, ANGUS, tenant in Dornie, 1770.
[NAS.E746.167.4]

MACLEOD, ANGUS, with his wife and three servants in
Duchlash, Assynt, Sutherland, 1774. [SA#79]

MCLEOD, ANGUS, in Duchlash, Assynt, Sutherland, 1774.
[SA#80]

MCLEOD, ANGUS, with his wife, one child, and one servant
in Elphine, Assynt, Sutherland, 1774. [SA#80]

MCLEOD, ANGUS MCCURCHY, wife, child, and a servant,
in Auchmore, Assynt, Sutherland, 1774. [SA#71]

MCLEOD, ANGUS MCALISTER, and wife, in Auchmore, Assynt, Sutherland, 1774. [SA#71]

MCLEOD, ANGUS MCINASH, with his wife, child, and one servant, in Culkein Achnacarnan, Assynt, Sutherland, 1774. [SA#78]

MCLEOD, ANGUS, with his wife, a child, and a servant, in Achnacarnan, Assynt, Sutherland, 1774. [SA#72]

MCLEOD, ANGUS, with his wife, and three children, in Clashmore, Assynt, Sutherland, 1774. [SA#75]

MCLEOD, ANGUS, in Clasnhessie, Assynt, Sutherland, 1774. [SA#76]

MCLEOD, ANGUS, with his wife, in Glenlerag, Assynt, Sutherland, 1774. [SA#80]

MCLEOD, or MCALISTER, ANGUS, a widower, with four children, in Culaig, Assynt, Sutherland, 1774. [SA#77]

MCLEOD, ANGUS BAIN, with his wife, three children, and one servant, in Knockan, Assynt, Sutherland, 1774. [SA#82]

MCLEOD, ANGUS DOW, in Culaig, Assynt, Sutherland, 1774. [SA#77]

MCLEOD, ANGUS DOW, with his wife, two children, and one servant, in Leadbeg, Assynt, Sutherland, 1774. [SA#83]

MACLEOD, ANGUS DOWN, with his wife, and four children, in Leadbeg, Assynt, Sutherland, 1774. [SA#83]

MCLEOD, ANGUS ROY, with his wife, and four children, in Knockan, Assynt, Sutherland, 1774. [SA#82]

MCLEOD, ANGUS ROY, with his wife, and two children, in Stronchrubie, Assynt, Sutherland, 1774. [SA#87]

MCLEOD, ANGUS, in Stronchrubie, Assynt, Sutherland, 1774. [SA#87]

MCLEOD, ANN, a widow, with three children, in Knockan, Assynt, Sutherland, 1774. [SA#83]

MCLEOD, ANNA, widow of Aeneas McLeod forester to the Earl of Cromarty, and her son Alexander McLeod, 1761. [NAS.E746.113.26/1]

MCLEOD, CHRISTIAN, widow of Hugh Ross, tenant in, Runabreake, 1770. [NAS.E746.167.5]

MCLEOD, CHRISTIAN, in Dornie, 1778. [NAS.E746.79]

MCLEOD, DAVID, sr., in Ledmore, a soldier in Captain Hugh McLeod of Geanies' Independent Company on 17 June 1746. [TGSI.LIII.380]

MCLEOD, DAVID, jr., in Ledmore, a soldier in Captain Hugh McLeod of Geanies Independent Company on 17 June 1746. [TGSI.LIII.380]

MCLEOD, DAVID, in Oldshoar, a soldier of Captain Hugh McKay's Independent Company in 1746. [TGSI.LIII.391]

MACLEOD, DONALD, in Plaid, soldier of George Munro of Culcairns' Independent Company, 1745. [TGSI.LIII.364]

MCLEOD, DONALD, sr., in Inchnadamph, Sutherland, a soldier in Captain Hugh McLeod of Geanies Independent Company on 17 June 1746. [TGSI.LIII.380]

MCLEOD, DONALD, in Stroncruby, a soldier in Captain Hugh McLeod of Geanies Independent Company on 17 June 1746. [TGSI.LIII.380]

MCLEOD, DONALD, jr., in Inchnadamph, Sutherland, a soldier in Captain Hugh McLeod of Geanies Independent Company on 17 June 1746. [TGSI.LIII.380]

MCLEOD, DONALD, in Cragain, a soldier of the Master of Ross' Independent Company at Linachan, 14 June 1746. [TGSI.LIII.392]

MCLEOD, DONALD, in Kergary, soldier of Captain Hugh McKay's Independent Company, 17 June 1746. [TGSI.LIII.390]

MACLEOD, DONALD, in Tongue, Sutherland, soldier of Captain George Mackay's Independent Company at Shiromore, 1746. [TGSI.LIII.371]

MACLEOD, DONALD, in Arduchow, soldier of Captain George Mackay's Independent Company at Shiromore, 1746. [TGSI.LIII.371]

MCLEOD, or MCHORKILL, DONALD, tenant in Dornie, 1754. [NAS.E746.113.4]

MCLEOD, DONALD, a tenant in Dalalvah, Halladale, Caithness, 1756. [NAS.GD87.SEC2.13]

MCLEOD, DONALD, tenant in Dornie, 1770. [NAS.E746.167.4]

MCLEOD, DONALD, tenant in Badentarbert, 1770. [NAS.E746.167.4]

MCLEOD, DONALD, with his wife and two children in Achmelvich, Assynt, Sutherland, 1774. [SA#71]

MCLEOD, DONALD, wife, and two children, in Badidarroch, Assynt, Sutherland, 1774. [SA#73]

MCLEOD, DONALD, wife, and child, in Auldnachy, Assynt, Sutherland, 1774. [SA#73]

MCLEOD, DONALD, with his wife, two children and one servant, in Culkin Drumbeg, Assynt, Sutherland, 1774. [SA#78]

MCLEOD, DONALD, with his wife, two children, and one servant in Duchlash, Assynt, Sutherland, 1774. [SA#80]

MCLEOD, or MCLEDICH, DONALD, with his wife, in Ardvar, Assynt, Sutherland, 1774. [SA#73]

MCLEOD, DONALD, with his wife and six children, in Balchladich, Assynt, Sutherland, 1774. [SA#74]

MCLEOD, DONALD, with his wife, in Clasnhessie, Assynt, Sutherland, 1774. [SA#76]

MCLEOD, DONALD, with his wife, two children, and one servant, in Camore, Kirkton, Assynt, Sutherland, 1774. [SA#82]

MCLEOD, or MCALISTER ROY, DONALD, with his wife, one child, and one servant in Culaig, Assynt, Sutherland, 1774. [SA#77]

MCLEOD, DONALD, with his wife, and two servants in Culaig, Assynt, Sutherland, 1774. [SA#77]

MCLEOD, DONALD, in Drumbeg, Assynt, Sutherland, 1774. [SA#79]

MCLEOD, or MCINNASH, DONALD, with his wife, and two children, in Clasnhessie, Assynt, Sutherland, 1774. [SA#76]

MCLEOD, DONALD, with his wife, in Ledmore, Assynt, Sutherland, 1774. [SA#84]

MCLEOD, DONALD MCRORY, a grasskeeper, with his wife, and three children, in Little Assynt, Sutherland, 1774. [SA#84]

MCLEOD, DONALD, with his wife, and four children, in Lochbannoch, Assynt, Sutherland, 1774. [SA#84]

MCLEOD, DONALD, with his wife, and three children, in Stronchrubie, Assynt, Sutherland, 1774. [SA#87]

MCLEOD, DONALD, with his wife, and one child, in Stronchrubie, Assynt, Sutherland, 1774. [SA#87]

MCLEOD, DUNCAN, in Tain, Easter Ross, 1766. [OR#409]

MCLEOD, DUNCAN, the elder, with his wife, four children, and one servant, in Culkein Achnacarnan, Assynt, Sutherland, 1774. [SA#78]

MCLEOD, DUNCAN, with his wife, and two children, in Edrachalda, Assynt, Sutherland, 1774. [SA#80]

MCLEOD, DUNCAN, with his wife, and three children, in Riancrevich, Leadmore, Assynt, Sutherland, 1774. [SA#83]

MCLEOD, or MCCURCHY, DUNCAN, with his wife, and child, in Culkein Achnacarnan, Assynt, Sutherland, 1774. [SA#78]

MCLEOD, or BAYNE, FLORE, with one servant, in Riancrevich, Ledmore, Assynt, Sutherland, 1774. [SA#84]

MACLEOD, HECTOR, soldier of Captain George Mackay's Independent Company at Shiromore, 1746. [TGSI.LIII.371]

MCLEOD, HUGH, in Cyderhall, soldier of Alexander Gunn's Independent Company at Shiromore, 16 June 1746. [TGSI.LIII.369]

MCLEOD, HUGH, in Achevirickle, a soldier in Captain Hugh McLeod of Geanies Independent Company on 17 June 1746. [TGSI.LIII.381]

MCLEOD, HUGH, in Torr, soldier of Captain Hugh McKay's Independent Company, 17 June 1746. [TGSI.LIII.390]

MCLEOD, HUGH, in Tongue, Sutherland, soldier of Captain Hugh McKay's Independent Company, 17 June 1746. [TGSI.LIII.390]

MCLEOD, HUGH, a soldier of Captain Hugh McKay's Independent Company in 1746. [TGSI.LIII.391]

MCLEOD, Captain, HUGH, of Geanies, Easter Ross, 1752. [NAS.RD4.178/2.453]

MCLEOD, HUGH, wife, and child, in Auldnachy, Assynt, Sutherland, 1774. [SA#73]

MCLEOD, HUGH, with his wife, and two servants, in Drumswordland, Assynt, Sutherland, 1774. [SA#79]

MCLEOD, or BAYNE, HUGH, with his wife, one child, and one servant, in Ledmore, Assynt, Sutherland, 1774. [SA#84]

MCLEOD, JAMES, in Coull, soldier of Captain Hugh McKay's Independent Company, 17 June 1746. [TGSI.LIII.390]

MACLEOD, JOHN, in Auchany, soldier of George Munro of Culcairns' Independent Company, 1745. [TGSI.LIII.364]

MACLEOD, JOHN, in Arskaig, soldier of George Munro of Culcairns' Independent Company, 1745. [TGSI.LIII.364]

MACLEOD, JOHN, in Bunrod, soldier of George Munro of Culcairns' Independent Company, 1745. [TGSI.LIII.364]

MCLEOD, JOHN, jr., in Knokan, a soldier in Captain Hugh McLeod of Geanies Independent Company on 17 June 1746. [TGSI.LIII.380]

MACLEOD, JOHN, soldier of Captain George Mackay's Independent Company at Shiromore, 1746. [TGSI.LIII.371]

MCLEOD, JOHN, in Elphine, a soldier in Captain Hugh McLeod of Geanies Independent Company on 17 June 1746. [TGSI.LIII.380]

MCLEOD, JOHN, in Achnagart, a soldier in Captain Hugh McLeod of Geanies Independent Company on 17 June 1746. [TGSI.LIII.380]

MCLEOD, JOHN, jr., in Oldny, a soldier in Captain Hugh McLeod of Geanies Independent Company on 17 June 1746. [TGSI.LIII.380]

MCLEOD, JOHN, in Drumbuig, a soldier in Captain Hugh McLeod of Geanies Independent Company on 17 June 1746. [TGSI.LIII.380]

MCLEOD, JOHN, in Kirktown, soldier of Captain Hugh McKay's Independent Company, 17 June 1746. [TGSI.LIII.390]

MCLEOD, JOHN, a drummer in Captain Hugh McLeod of Geanies Independent Company on 17 June 1746. [TGSI.LIII.380]

MCLEOD, JOHN, in Altas, a soldier in Captain Hugh McLeod of Geanies Independent Company on 17 June 1746. [TGSI.LIII.381]

MCLEOD, JOHN, jr., soldier of Captain Hugh McKay's Independent Company, 17 June 1746. [TGSI.LIII.390]

MCLEOD, JOHN, in Little Altas, a soldier in Captain Hugh McLeod of Geanies Independent Company on 17 June 1746. [TGSI.LIII.381]

MCLEOD, JOHN, a tenant on the Cromarty Estate in 1745, prisoner of the Jacobites, escaped and joined Captain McLeod of Geanies Independent Company, a resident in Kenchilish 1756. [NAS.E746.113.7]

MCLEOD, JOHN, in Tain, Easter Ross, 1766. [OR#409]

MCLEOD, JOHN, with his wife, and five children, in Clasnhessie, Assynt, Sutherland, 1774. [SA#76]

MCLEOD, JOHN, and wife, in Achmelvich, Assynt, Sutherland, 1774. [SA#71]

MCLEOD, JOHN, with his wife, in Dearlan, Auchmore, Assynt, Sutherland, 1774. [SA#72]

MCLEOD, JOHN, with his wife, three children, and a servant, in Brakloch, Assynt, Sutherland, 1774. [SA#74]

MCLEOD, JOHN, with his wife, child, and two servants, in Clachtole, Assynt, Sutherland, 1774. [SA#74]

MCLEOD, JOHN, miller, with his wife, three children and three servants, in Clasnhessie, Assynt, Sutherland, 1774. [SA#76]

MCLEOD, JOHN, with his wife, four children, and two servants, in Drumswordland, Assynt, Sutherland, 1774. [SA#79]

MCLEOD, JOHN, with his wife, two children, and one servant, in Drumbeg, Assynt, Sutherland, 1774. [SA#79]

MACLEOD, JOHN, with his wife, one child, and one servant, in Duchlash, Assynt, Sutherland, 1774. [SA#79]

MCLEOD, JOHN BAIN, with his wife, and two children, in Glaskoil, Leadmore, Assynt, Sutherland, 1774. [SA#83]

MCLEOD, JOHN DOW, with his wife, and one servant, in Leadbeg, Assynt, Sutherland, 1774. [SA#83]

MCLEOD, or MCONEIL, JOHN, with his wife and two children, in Achmelvich, Assynt, Sutherland, 1774. [SA#71]

MCLEOD, or MCHORMAD, JOHN, with his wife and three children, in Achmelvich, Assynt, Sutherland, 1774. [SA#71]

MCLEOD, or MCKENNETH, JOHN, with his wife, and three children, in Clachtole, Assynt, Sutherland, 1774. [SA#74]

MCLEOD, or MCNEIL, JOHN, with his wife, two children and one servant, in Clasnhessie, Assynt, Sutherland, 1774. [SA#76]

MCLEOD, or MCHORMAD OG, JOHN, with his wife, and four servants, in Culkin Drumbeg, Assynt, Sutherland, 1774. [SA#79]

MCLEOD, JOHN ROY, with his wife, and three children, in Ledmore, Assynt, Sutherland, 1774. [SA#84]

MCLEOD, JOHN, with his wife, and three children, in Torbreck, Assynt, Sutherland, 1774. [SA#87]

MCLEOD, JOHN, sr., in Oldny, a soldier in Captain Hugh McLeod of Geanies Independent Company on 17 June 1746. [TGSI.LIII.380]

MCLEOD, KATHARINE, a widow, and two children, in Auldnachy, Assynt, Sutherland, 1774. [SA#73]

MCLEOD, KATHARINE, with her daughter, in Badinamban, Assynt, Sutherland, 1774. [SA#74]

MCLEOD, KATHARINE, a widow with her daughter, in Balchladich, Assynt, Sutherland, 1774. [SA#74]

MCLEOD, KENNETH, in Inver, a soldier in Captain Hugh McLeod of Geanies Independent Company on 17 June 1746. [TGSI.LIII.380]

MCLEOD, KENNETH, in Culkin Drumbeg, Assynt, Sutherland, 1774. [SA#79]

MCLEOD, KENNETH, with his wife, one child, and two servants, in Inverkirkaig, Assynt, Sutherland, 1774. [SA#81]

MCLEOD, or ROY, KENNETH, wife, and two servants, in Badidarroch, Assynt, Sutherland, 1774. [SA#73]

MCLEOD, KENNETH, with his wife, one child and one servants, in Stoer, Assynt, Sutherland, 1774. [SA#86]

MCLEOD, MARGARET, with five children, and two servants, in Drumbeg, Assynt, Sutherland, 1774. [SA#79]

MCLEOD, MARY, a tenant in Halladale, Caithness, 1756. [NAS.GD87.SEC2.13]

MCLEOD, MURDO, in Amat, a soldier in Captain Hugh McLeod of Geanies Independent Company on 17 June 1746. [TGSI.LIII.380]

MCLEOD, MURDO, a sergeant in Captain Hugh McLeod of Geanies Independent Company on 17 June 1746. [TGSI.LIII.380]

MCLEOD, MURDO, a drummer in Captain Hugh McLeod of Geanies Independent Company on 17 June 1746. [TGSI.LIII.380]

MCLEOD, MURDO, with his wife, and four children, in Clachtole, Assynt, Sutherland, 1774. [SA#74]

MCLEOD, MURDO, in Clachtole, Assynt, Sutherland, 1774. [SA#74]

MCLEOD, MURDOCH, tenant in Badentarbert, 1770. [NAS.E746.167.4]

MCLEOD, MURDOCH, tenant in Runabreake, 1770. [NAS.E746.167.5]

MCLEOD, MURDOCH, wife, and two children, in Auchmore, Assynt, Sutherland, 1774. [SA#71]

MCLEOD, MURDOCH, with his wife, two children, and one servant, in Drumswordland, Assynt, Sutherland, 1774. [SA#79]

MCLEOD, MURDOCH, at Bracklach of Leadbeg, with his wife, and three servants, 1774. [SA#83]

MCLEOD, MURDOCH, with his wife, and three children, in Leadmore, Assynt, Sutherland, 1774. [SA#83]

MCLEOD, or MCCURCHY, MURDOCH, with his wife and two servants, in Badinamban, Assynt, Sutherland, 1774. [SA#74]

MCLEOD, NEIL, tenant in Dornie, 1770. [NAS.E746.167.4]

MCLEOD, NEIL, with his wife, three children and one servant, in Clasnhessie, Assynt, Sutherland, 1774. [SA#76]

MCLEOD, NEIL, with his wife, and two servants, in Knockan, Assynt, Sutherland, 1774. [SA#82]

MCLEOD, NEIL, with his wife, and one child, in Ledmore, Assynt, Sutherland, 1774. [SA#84]

MCLEOD, or MCINNASHDOWN, NEIL, with his wife and four children, in Badinamban, Assynt, Sutherland, 1774. [SA#74]

MCLEOD, NEILL, in Dibidell, a soldier of the Master of Ross' Independent Company at Linachan, 14 June 1746. [TGSI.LIII.392]

MCLEOD, NORMAN, with his wife, in Achmelvich, Assynt, Sutherland, 1774. [SA#71]

MCLEOD, NORMAND, in Strathmelness, soldier of Captain George Mackay's Independent Company at Shiromore, 1746. [TGSI.LIII.371]

MCLEOD, NORMAND, with his wife, and child, in Clachtole, Assynt, Sutherland, 1774. [SA#74]

MCLEOD, NORMAND, with his wife, three children, and one servant, in Inverkirkaig, Assynt, Sutherland, 1774. [SA#80]

MCLEOD, NORMAND, with his wife, and two children, in Culin, Kirkton, Assynt, Sutherland, 1774. [SA#82]

MCLEOD, NORMAND, with his wife, four children, and one servant, in Leadmore, Assynt, Sutherland, 1774. [SA#83]

MCLEOD, or MCCONIL, NORMAND, with his wife, child, and one servant, in Culkein Achnacarnan, Assynt, Sutherland, 1774. [SA#78]

MCLEOD, ROBERT, in Coull, soldier of Captain Hugh McKay's Independent Company, 17 June 1746. [TGSI.LIII.390]

MCLEOD, ROBERT, with his wife, four children, and two servants, in Layne, Assynt, Sutherland, 1774. [SA#84]

MCLEOD, RODERICK, of Cadboll, Easter Ross, 1733. [NAS.RD4.178/1.16]

MCLEOD, RODERICK, tenant in Rive of Coigach, 1756. [NAS.E746.113.10/1]

MCLEOD, RODERICK, in Rive, 1756. [NAS.E746/79]

MCLEOD, RODERICK, born 1703, tacksman of Forsinaird, died 1761. [Kirkton gravestone, Melvich, Sutherland]

MCLEOD, RODERICK, tenant in Runabreake, 1770. [NAS.E746.167.5]

MCLEOD, RODERICK, with his wife and two children, in Auchmore, Assynt, Sutherland, 1774. [SA#72]

MCLEOD, RODERICK, with his wife, four children, and one servant in Culaig, Assynt, Sutherland, 1774. [SA#77]

MCLEOD, RODERICK, son of Roderick McLeod, with his wife, in Knocknach, Assynt, Sutherland, 1774. [SA#76]

MCLEOD, RODERICK, with his wife, two children, and two servants in Duchlash, Assynt, Sutherland, 1774. [SA#80]

MCLEOD, or KILE, RODERICK, with his wife, and two children, in Culaig, Assynt, Sutherland, 1774. [SA#77]

MCLEOD, or MCANGUS, RODERICK, with his wife, two children, and two servants in Knocknach, Assynt, Sutherland, 1774. [SA#76]

MACLEOD, RODERICK, with his wife, six children and one servant, in Unapool, Assynt, Sutherland, 1774. [SA#88]

MCLEOD, RODERICK, alias RORY BAIN, with his wife, and one servant, in Knockan, Assynt, Sutherland, 1774. [SA#82]

MACLEOD, RODERICK, of Cadboll, Easter Ross, 1750. [NAS.E746.4]

MCLEOD, RORY, in Achnaheglish, a soldier in Captain Hugh McLeod of Geanies Independent Company on 17 June 1746. [TGSI.LIII.380]

MCLEOD, RORY, in Store, a soldier in Captain Hugh McLeod of Geanies Independent Company on 17 June 1746. [TGSI.LIII.380]

MCLEOD, RORY, soldier of Captain Hugh McKay's Independent Company, 17 June 1746. [TGSI.LIII.390]

MCLEOD, RORY, with his wife, and four children, in Clashmore, Assynt, Sutherland, 1774. [SA#75]

MCLEOD, RORY, with his wife and two servants in Knocknach, Assynt, Sutherland, 1774. [SA#76]

MCLEOD, or JOHNSON, RORY, in Knocknach, Assynt, Sutherland, 1774. [SA#76]

MCLEOD, RORY or RODERICK, the younger, with his wife, and one child, in Ledmore, Assynt, Sutherland, 1774. [SA#84]

MCLEOD, RORY ROY, with his wife, one child, and one servant, in Ledmore, Assynt, Sutherland, 1774. [SA#84]

MCLEOD, THOMAS, in Langle, a soldier of the Master of Ross' Independent Company at Linachan, 14 June 1746. [TGSI.LIII.392]

MCLEOD, WILLIAM, in Achintoule, a soldier in Captain Hugh McLeod of Geanies Independent Company on 17 June 1746. [TGSI.LIII.381]

MACLEOD, WILLIAM, soldier of Captain George Mackay's Independent Company at Shiromore, 1746. [TGSI.LIII.371]

MCLEOD, WILLIAM, in Knockbreck, soldier of Captain Hugh McKay's Independent Company, 17 June 1746. [TGSI.LIII.390]

MCLEOD, WILLIAM, in Torr, soldier of Captain Hugh McKay's Independent Company, 17 June 1746. [TGSI.LIII.391]

MCLEOD, WILLIAM, with his wife, and six children, in Clasnhessie, Assynt, Sutherland, 1774. [SA#76]

MCLEOD, WILLIAM, with his wife, in Drumswordland, Assynt, Sutherland, 1774. [SA#79]

MCLEOD, WILLIAM ROY, with his wife and one servant in Duchlash, Assynt, Sutherland, 1774. [SA#80]

MCLEOD, or MCEAN, WILLIAM, with his wife, two children, and a servant, in Clachtole, Assynt, Sutherland, 1774.
[SA#74]

MCLEOD, Mrs, widow of Erick McLeod, with two children, in Stoer, Assynt, Sutherland, 1774. [SA#86]

MCLEOD, ..., of Talisker, Captain of an Independent Company commanded by the Earl of Loudoun at Dornoch, Sutherland, 10 March 1746. [MCP.V.31]

MCLEOD, ..., of Waterstyn, Captain of an Independent Company commanded by the Earl of Loudoun at Dornoch, Sutherland, 10 March 1746. [MCP.V.31]

MCLEOD, ..., of Geanies, Captain of an Independent Company commanded by the Earl of Loudoun at Dornoch, Sutherland, 10 March 1746. [MCP.V.31]

MCLEY, FARQUHAR, in Strathchonnan, soldier of Captain Alexander Mackenzie's Independent Company, deserted in 1746. [TGSI.LIII.382]

MCLEY, MURDOCH, in Bonar, a soldier of the Master of Ross' Independent Company at Linachan, 14 June 1746. [TGSI.LIII.392]

MCLEY, MURDOCH, in Keanloch, soldier of Captain Colin Mackenzie's Independent Company, 1746. [TGSI.LIII.384]

MCLINNAN, FARQUHAR, in Achyark, soldier of Captain Colin Mackenzie's Independent Company, 1746. [TGSI.LIII.384]

MCLINNAN, MALCOLM, in Evelacks, soldier of Alexander Gunn's Independent Company at Shiromore, 16 June 1746. [TGSI.LIII.369]

MACMARTIN, RORIE, soldier of Captain Alexander Mackenzie's Independent Company, 1746. [TGSI.LIII.382]

MACMITCHELL, NORMAN, in Tain, Easter Ross, 1766. [OR#409]

MCNEIL, or MCLEOD, ANGUS, a bachelor, in Knockan, Assynt, Sutherland, 1774. [SA#83]

MCNEIL, DONALD OIG, in Sheldack, Applecross, Wester Ross, 1718. [TGSI.LIV.452]

MCNEIL, JOHN RORY, with his wife, and six children, in Stoer, Assynt, Sutherland, 1774. [SA#86]

MCNEILL, JOHN KER, with his wife and child, in Achmelvich, Assynt, Sutherland, 1774. [SA#71]

MCNEILL, RODERICK MCKENZIE, with his wife, and child, in Culkein Achnacarnan, Assynt, Sutherland, 1774. [SA#78]

MACNIVEN, DONALD, in Dornie, soldier of Captain Colin Mackenzie's Independent Company, 1746. [TGSI.LIII.384]

MCNOON, RODERICK, a shoemaker in Tain, Easter Ross, 1766. [OR#409]

MCNORMOID, FINLAY, soldier of Captain Alexander Mackenzie's Independent Company, 1746. [TGSI.LIII.382]

MCOIL, ALEXANDER OIG, in Auchnadroil, Applecross, Wester Ross, 1718. [TGSI.LIV.451]

MCOIL, DONALD OIG, in Cullnokill, Applecross, Wester Ross, 1718. [TGSI.LIV.452]

MCOIL, DONALD VICERQR VICINISH VICEAN, in Rishell, Applecross, Wester Ross, 1718. [TGSI.LIV.450]

MCOIL, FINLAY VANE, in Kirkton of Applecross, Wester Ross, 1718. [TGSI.LIV.451]

MCOIL, JOHN VICUNLEY, in Sheldack, Applecross, Wester Ross, 1718. [TGSI.LIV.452]

MCOIL, JOHN DUY, in Lagginteamore, Applecross, Wester Ross, 1718. [TGSI.LIV.450]

MCOIL, RORY VICRORY, in Rushell, Applecross, Wester Ross, 1718. [TGSI.LIV.450]

MCOISEA, W., in Tain, Easter Ross, 1766. [OR#409]

MCONELL, ANGUS, in Rishell, Applecross, Wester Ross, 1718. [TGSI.LIV.450]

MACONELL, DUNCAN, in Ballogie, Applecross, Wester Ross, 1718. [TGSI.LIV.452]

MCORMET, KENNETH, in Langwell, Applecross, Wester Ross, 1718. [TGSI.LIV.451]

MCOWELL, JOHN, a weaver in Tain, Easter Ross, 1766. [OR#409]

MCPHADRICK, DONALD, soldier of Captain George Mackay's Independent Company at Shiromore, 1746. [TGSI.LIII.371]

MCPHAIL, HECTOR, born Inverness 1716, educated at King's College, Aberdeen, minister of Resolis, Ross and Cromarty, from 1748 to 1774, died 23 January 1784. Husband of (1) Elizabeth, daughter of John Balfour minister of Nigg, parents of Isobel; (2) Anne Cuthbert, parents of Jean, Paul, Magdalene, George, James, Elizabeth, and William. [F.7.19]

MCPHEN, KATHARINE, a cottar in Mey, Caithness, 1771. [NAS.GD96.679.14]

MCPHERSON, ALEXANDER, a tenant in Halladale, Caithness, 1756. [NAS.GD87.SEC2.13]

MCPHERSON, ALEXANDER, a shoemaker in Tain, Easter Ross, 1766. [OR#409]

MCPHERSON, ANGUS, in Novar, soldier of George Munro of Culcairns' Independent Company, 1745. [TGSI.LIII.364]

MCPHERSON, DONALD, in Knockarball, soldier of Alexander Gunn's Independent Company at Shiromore, 16 June 1746. [TGSI.LIII.369]

MCPHERSON, DONALD, in Dalhalow, soldier of Captain Hugh McKay's Independent Company, 17 June 1746. [TGSI.LIII.390]

MCPHERSON, DONALD, a tenant in Delalvah, Halladale, Caithness, 1756. [NAS.GD87.SEC2.13]

MCPHERSON, HUGH, soldier of Captain Hugh McKay's Independent Company, 17 June 1746. [TGSI.LIII.390]

MCPHERSON, JOHN, a tenant in Halladale, Caithness, 1756. [NAS.GD87.SEC2.13]

MACPHERSON, MARTIN, born 1723 son of John MacPherson schoolmaster at Orbost, Skye, minister of Golspie, Sutherland, from 1754 to 1773, died on 10 September 1773, husband of Elizabeth Gordon, parents of twelve children. [F.7.87]

MCPHERSON, MURDOCH, soldier of Alexander Gunn's Independent Company at Shiromore, 16 June 1746. [TGSI.LIII.369]

MCPHERSON, MURDOCH, a tenant in Halladale, Caithness, 1756. [NAS.GD87.SEC2.13]

MCPHERSON, WILLIAM, a shoemaker in Tain, Easter Ross, 1766. [OR#409]

MCPHERSON, WILLIAM, in Tain, Easter Ross, 1766. [OR#409]

MACQUAN, DONALD, soldier of Captain Alexander Mackenzie's Independent Company, dead by 1746. [TGSI.LIII.382]

MACQUAN, DUNCAN, in Strathconon, Ross and Cromarty, soldier of Captain Colin Mackenzie's Independent Company, 1746. [TGSI.LIII.385]

MACQUAN, JOHN, soldier of Captain Alexander Mackenzie's Independent Company, dead by 1746. [TGSI.LIII.382]

MACRA, ALEXANDER, tacksman of Letterfern, 1766. [NAS.GD46.SEC.1/212]

MACRA, FARQUHAR, tacksman of Lochalsh, 1766, and of Cro and Letterfern, 1766. [NAS.GD46.SEC.1/212]

MACRA, JOHN, tacksman of Lochalsh, 1766. [NAS.GD46.SEC.1/212]

MCRAE, ALEXANDER, born 1644, resident of Bailon, died 1724. [Lochbroom, Ross and Cromarty, gravestone]

MCRAE, ALEXANDER, soldier of Captain Alexander Mackenzie's Independent Company, dead by 1746. [TGSI.LIII.382]

MCRAE, ALEXANDER, in Achladorlan, soldier of Captain Alexander Mackenzie's Independent Company, 1746. [TGSI.LIII.383]

MCRAE, DONALD, the elder, in Nedd, Assynt, Sutherland, 1774. [SA#85]

MCRAE, DONALD, in Nedd, Assynt, Sutherland, 1774. [SA#85]

MCRAE, DONALD, with his wife, and seven others, in Unapool, Assynt, Sutherland, 1774. [SA#88]

MCRAE, DUNCAN, in Applecross, Wester Ross, a soldier of Captain Alexander Mackenzie's Independent Company, 1746. [TGSI.LIII.382]

MCRAE, DUNCAN, at Tain mills, Easter Ross, 1766. [OR#409]

MCRAE, DUNCAN, born 1732, died 1832, husband of Mary Kennedy. [Applecross, Wester Ross, gravestone]

MCRAE, FARQUHAR, soldier of Captain Alexander Mackenzie's Independent Company, 1746. [TGSI.LIII.382]

MACRAE, FINLAY, soldier of Captain Alexander Mackenzie's Independent Company, dead by 1746. [TGSI.LIII.382]

MACRAE, JOHN, in Salchy, soldier of Captain Alexander Mackenzie's Independent Company, 1746. [TGSI.LIII.383]

MCRAE, JOHN, soldier of Captain Alexander Mackenzie's Independent Company, dead by 1746. [TGSI.LIII.382]

MCRAE, JOHN, in Nedd, Assynt, Sutherland, 1774. [SA#85]

MCRAE, KENNETH, Dundonell, buried 12 February 1732. [Loch Broom, Sutherland, gravestone]

MCRAE, KENNETH, at Tain mills, Easter Ross, 1766. [OR#409]

MCRAE, KENNETH, in Nedd, Assynt, Sutherland, 1774. [SA#85]

MACRAE, MURDO, with his wife, one child, and three servants, in Glenlerag, Assynt, Sutherland, 1774. [SA#80]

MACRATH, ALEXANDER, in Achinshean, soldier of Captain Colin Mackenzie's Independent Company, 1746. [TGSI.LIII.384]

MACRATH, ALEXANDER, in Drugage, soldier of Captain Colin Mackenzie's Independent Company, 1746. [TGSI.LIII.384]

MACRATH, ALEXANDER, in Invershein, soldier of Captain Colin Mackenzie's Independent Company, 1746. [TGSI.LIII.384]

MACRATH, ARCHIBALD, in Achindraen, soldier of Captain Colin Mackenzie's Independent Company, 1746. [TGSI.LIII.384]

MACRATH, CHRISTOPHER, in Inchlongrat, soldier of Captain Colin Mackenzie's Independent Company, 1746.
[TGSI.LIII.384]

MACRATH, DONALD, sergeant of Captain Colin Mackenzie's Independent Company, 1746.
[TGSI.LIII.384]

MACRATH, DONALD, in Inverinate, soldier of Captain Colin Mackenzie's Independent Company, 1746.
[TGSI.LIII.384]

MACRATH, DONALD, in Kirkton, soldier of Captain Colin Mackenzie's Independent Company, 1746.
[TGSI.LIII.384]

MACRATH, DONALD, in Inige, soldier of Captain Colin Mackenzie's Independent Company, 1746.
[TGSI.LIII.384]

MACRATH, DONALD, in Inchcroe, soldier of Captain Colin Mackenzie's Independent Company, 1746.
[TGSI.LIII.384]

MACRATH, DONALD, in Lealt, soldier of Captain Colin Mackenzie's Independent Company, 1746.
[TGSI.LIII.384]

MACRATH, DONALD, in Inverinate, soldier of Captain Colin Mackenzie's Independent Company, 1746.
[TGSI.LIII.384]

MACRATH, DONALD, in Cambuslynie, soldier of Captain Colin Mackenzie's Independent Company, 1746.
[TGSI.LIII.385]

MACRATH, DONALD, in Shearwall, soldier of Captain Colin Mackenzie's Independent Company, 1746.
[TGSI.LIII.385]

MACRATH, DUNCAN, in Inverinate, soldier of Captain Colin Mackenzie's Independent Company, 1746.
[TGSI.LIII.384]

MACRATH, DUNCAN, in Kinalort, soldier of Captain Colin Mackenzie's Independent Company, 1746.
[TGSI.LIII.384]

MACRATH, DUNCAN, in Kirkton, soldier of Captain Colin Mackenzie's Independent Company, 1746.
[TGSI.LIII.384]

MACRATH, DUNCAN, in Radigan, soldier of Captain Colin Mackenzie's Independent Company, 1746.
[TGSI.LIII.384]

MACRATH, DUNCAN, in Beolage, soldier of Captain Colin Mackenzie's Independent Company, 1746.
[TGSI.LIII.384]

MACRATH, FARQUHAR, corporal of Captain Colin Mackenzie's Independent Company, 1746.
[TGSI.LIII.384]

MACRATH, FINLAY, in Achyouran, soldier of Captain Colin Mackenzie's Independent Company, 1746.
[TGSI.LIII.384]

MACRATH, FINLAY, in Buncaloch, soldier of Captain Colin Mackenzie's Independent Company, 1746.
[TGSI.LIII.384]

MACRATH, JOHN, in Inverinate, soldier of Captain Colin Mackenzie's Independent Company, 1746.
[TGSI.LIII.384]

MACRATH, JOHN, in Mamage, soldier of Captain Colin Mackenzie's Independent Company, 1746.
[TGSI.LIII.384]

MACRATH, JOHN, in Dornie, soldier of Captain Colin Mackenzie's Independent Company, 1746.
[TGSI.LIII.384]

MACRATH, JOHN, in Achingart, soldier of Captain Colin Mackenzie's Independent Company, 1746.
[TGSI.LIII.384]

MACRATH, JOHN, sergeant of Captain Colin Mackenzie's Independent Company, 1746. [TGSI.LIII.384]

MACRATH, JOHN, in Inverinate, soldier of Captain Colin Mackenzie's Independent Company, 1746.
[TGSI.LIII.384]

MACRATH, JOHN, in Rappash, soldier of Captain Colin Mackenzie's Independent Company, 1746.
[TGSI.LIII.384]

MACRATH, JOHN, in Inchcroe, soldier of Captain Colin Mackenzie's Independent Company, 1746.
[TGSI.LIII.384]

MACRATH, JOHN, in Carr, soldier of Captain Colin Mackenzie's Independent Company, 1746.
[TGSI.LIII.384]

MACRATH, JOHN, in Rourach, soldier of Captain Colin Mackenzie's Independent Company, 1746.
[TGSI.LIII.384]

MACRATH, JOHN, in Dornie, soldier of Captain Colin Mackenzie's Independent Company, 1746.
[TGSI.LIII.384]

MACRATH, JOHN, in Achintyart, soldier of Captain Colin Mackenzie's Independent Company, 1746.
[TGSI.LIII.384]

MACRATH, JOHN, in Little Oassie, soldier of Captain Colin Mackenzie's Independent Company, 1746.
[TGSI.LIII.385]

MACRATH, JOHN, in Blarnebie, soldier of Captain Colin Mackenzie's Independent Company, 1746.
[TGSI.LIII.385]

MACRATH, MALCOLM, in Mamark, soldier of Captain Colin Mackenzie's Independent Company, 1746. [TGSI.LIII.384]

MCRATH, MURDOCH, in Main, soldier of Captain Colin Mackenzie's Independent Company, 1746. [TGSI.LIII.385]

MACRATH, MURDOCH, brother of John in Dornie, soldier of Captain Colin Mackenzie's Independent Company, 1746. [TGSI.LIII.384]

MACRATH, MURDOCH, in Inverinate, soldier of Captain Colin Mackenzie's Independent Company, 1746. [TGSI.LIII.384]

MACRATH, RORIE, in Glenlinge, soldier of Captain Colin Mackenzie's Independent Company, 1746. [TGSI.LIII.384]

MACRATH, THOMAS, in Inverinate, soldier of Captain Colin Mackenzie's Independent Company, 1746. [TGSI.LIII.384]

MACRICHIE, KENNETH, soldier of Captain Alexander Mackenzie's Independent Company, 1746. [TGSI.LIII.383]

MACRORY, ANGUS MCLEOD, with his wife, in Leadbeg, Assynt, Sutherland, 1774. [SA#83]

MCRORY, ANGUS, in Clashmore, Assynt, Sutherland, 1774. [SA#75]

MCRORY, JOHN MCLEOD, with his wife, three children and one servant, in Stoer, and Torbreck, Assynt, Sutherland, 1774. [SA#86]

MACRORY, or MCLEOD, NEIL, with his wife, one child, and one servant in Culaig, Assynt, Sutherland, 1774. [SA#77]

MCSTIVEN, DONALD, sr., in Tain, Easter Ross, 1766.
[OR#409]

MACTARLICH, JOHN, in Kirkton, soldier of Captain Alexander Mackenzie's Independent Company, 1746.
[TGSI.LIII.383]

MCTHORMAD, or MCLEOD, ANGUS, a widower, with three children, and one servant, in Knockan, Assynt, Sutherland, 1774. [SA#83]

MCULAY, DUNCAN, in Glas, soldier of Captain Alexander Mackenzie's Independent Company, 1746.
[TGSI.LIII.382]

MCUNLEY, DONALD, in Rishell, Applecross, Wester Ross, 1718. [TGSI.LIV.450]

MCUNLEY, MURDO, in Kirkton of Applecross, Wester Ross, 1718. [TGSI.LIV.451]

MCURCHIE, DONALD, in Ardoch, soldier of George Munro of Culcairns' Independent Company, 1745.
[TGSI.LIII.364]

MACURCHIE, DUNCAN, in Ballogie, Applecross, Wester Ross, 1718. [TGSI.LIV.452]

MCURCHY, FARQUHAR, (1), in Langwell, Applecross, Wester Ross, 1718. [TGSI.LIV.451]

MCURCHY, FARQUHAR, (2), in Langwell, Applecross, Wester Ross, 1718. [TGSI.LIV.451]

MCURCHY, NORMAND, in Owagan, Applecross, Wester Ross,, 1718. [TGSI.LIV.452]

MCURCHY, WILLIAM, in Owagan, Applecross, Wester Ross,, 1718. [TGSI.LIV.452]

MACWILL, JOHN R., a weaver in Tain, Easter Ross, 1766.
[OR#409]

MCWILLIAM, ALEXANDER, in Knockbean, soldier of Captain Colin Mackenzie's Independent Company, 1746. [TGSI.LIII.384]

MCWILLIAM, ANGUS ROSS, in Tain, Easter Ross, a soldier of the Master of Ross' Independent Company at Linachan, 14 June 1746. [TGSI.LIII.392]

MCWILLIAM, DAVID R., a weaver in Tain, Easter Ross, 1766. [OR#409]

MCWILLIAM, FINLAY, in Tain, Easter Ross, 1766. [OR#409]

MCWILLIAM, JOHN, a weaver in Tain, Easter Ross, 1766. [OR#409]

MCWILLIAM, KENNETH, in Lagmacop, Applecross, Wester Ross, 1718. [TGSI.LIV.450]

MCWILLIAM, KENNETH, in Achlonacon, soldier of Captain Colin Mackenzie's Independent Company, 1746. [TGSI.LIII.384]

MCWILLIAM, KENNETH, in Balinauld, soldier of Captain Colin Mackenzie's Independent Company, 1746. [TGSI.LIII.384]

MCWILLIAM, NEIL, in Rishell, Applecross, Wester Ross, 1718. [TGSI.LIV.450]

MCWILLIAM, THOMAS, in Tain, Easter Ross, 1766. [OR#409]

MANSON, ALEXANDER, tenant in Eastside of Mey, Caithness, 1771. [NAS.GD96.679.14]

MANSON, DAVID, a shoemaker in Tain, Easter Ross, 1766. [OR#409]

MANSON, FINLAY, a shoemaker in Tain, Easter Ross, 1766. [OR#409]

MANSON, JOHN, a cottar in Mey, Caithness, 1771. [NAS.GD96.679.14]

MANSON, RODERICK, a cottar in Gills, Mey, Caithness, 1771. [NAS.GD96.679.14]

MANSON, WILLIAM, a cottar in Mey, Caithness, 1771. [NAS.GD96.679.14]

MASON, ROBERT, sailor or fisherman settled at New Tarbat, Easter Ross, 1765. [NAS.E746.80]

MATHESON, ALEXANDER, in Farnaig, soldier of Captain Alexander Mackenzie's Independent Company, 1746. [TGSI.LIII.383]

MATHESON, ALEXANDER, tacksman of Lochalsh, 1766. [NAS.GD46.SEC.1/212]

MATHESON, DAVID, Sergeant of Captain Alexander Mackenzie's Independent Company, 1746. [TGSI.LIII.382]

MATHESON, DAVID, in Durinish, soldier of Captain Alexander Mackenzie's Independent Company, dead by 1746. [TGSI.LIII.383]

MATHESON, DONALD, in Frie, soldier of Alexander Gunn's Independent Company at Shiromore, 16 June 1746. [TGSI.LIII.369]

MATHESON, DONALD, in Achnadarrach, soldier of Captain Alexander Mackenzie's Independent Company, 1746. [TGSI.LIII.383]

MATHESON, DONALD, in Farnaig, soldier of Captain Alexander Mackenzie's Independent Company, 1746. [TGSI.LIII.383]

MATHESON, DONALD, tacksman of Lochalsh, 1766. [NAS.GD46.SEC.1/212]

MATHESON, DUNCAN, in Farnaig, soldier of Captain Alexander Mackenzie's Independent Company, 1746. [TGSI.LIII.383]

MATHESON, JOHN, sergeant of Alexander Gunn's Independent Company at Shiromore, 16 June 1746. [TGSI.LIII.369]

MATHESON, JOHN, in Midstrome, soldier of Captain Alexander Mackenzie's Independent Company, 1746. [TGSI.LIII.382]

MATHESON, JOHN, in Slumbey, soldier of Captain Alexander Mackenzie's Independent Company, 1746. [TGSI.LIII.382]

MATHESON, JOHN, in Farnaig, soldier of Captain Alexander Mackenzie's Independent Company, 1746. [TGSI.LIII.383]

MATHESON, JOHN BAYN, soldier of Captain Alexander Mackenzie's Independent Company, dead by 1746. [TGSI.LIII.382]

MATHESON, JOHN DOW, in Rudow, soldier of Captain Alexander Mackenzie's Independent Company, 1746. [TGSI.LIII.382]

MATHESON, JOHN, in Garr, soldier of Captain Alexander Mackenzie's Independent Company, 1746. [TGSI.LIII.382]

MATHESON, JOHN, schoolmaster in the barony of New Tarbat, Easter Ross, 1760s. [NAS.E746.85/117]

MATHESON, JOHN, tacksman of Lochalsh, Durinish, 1766. [NAS.GD46.SEC.1/212]

MATHESON, KEN, soldier of Captain Alexander Mackenzie's Independent Company, 1746. [TGSI.LIII.383]

MATHESON, KENNETH, corporal of Captain Alexander
Mackenzie's Independent Company, 1746.
[TGSI.LIII.382]

MATHESON, KENNETH, in Braintsan, soldier of Captain
Alexander Mackenzie's Independent Company, 1746.
[TGSI.LIII.383]

MATHESON, KENNETH, in Ardnarff, soldier of Captain
Alexander Mackenzie's Independent Company, dead by
1746. [TGSI.LIII.382]

MATHESON, KENNETH, in Balmacara, soldier of Captain
Alexander Mackenzie's Independent Company, 1746.
[TGSI.LIII.382]

MATHESON, KENNETH, tacksman of Lochalsh, 1766.
[NAS.GD46.SEC.1/212]

MATHESON, KENNETH, a shoemaker in Tain, Easter Ross,
1766. [OR#409]

MATHESON, KENNETH, with his mother, his sister, and
one servant, in Nedd, Assynt, Sutherland, 1774. [SA#85]

MATHESON, MURDO, soldier of Captain Alexander
Mackenzie's Independent Company, 1746.
[TGSI.LIII.382]

MATHESON, MURDO, tacksman of Lochalsh, Wester Ross,
1766. [NAS.GD46.SEC.1/212]

MATHESON, NEIL, in Frie, soldier of Alexander Gunn's
Independent Company at Shiromore, 16 June 1746.
[TGSI.LIII.369]

MATHESON, NEILL, soldier of Captain George Mackay's
Independent Company at Shiromore, 1746.
[TGSI.LIII.371]

MATHESON, NIEL, in Balvraid, soldier of Alexander
Gunn's Independent Company at Shiromore, 16 June
1746. [TGSI.LIII.369]

MATHESON, WILLIAM, in Store, a soldier in Captain Hugh McLeod of Geanies Independent Company on 17 June 1746. [TGSI.LIII.380]

MATHEWSON, DOUGALL, in Glen, Applecross, Wester Ross,, 1718. [TGSI.LIV.451]

MATHIESON, ANGUS, with his wife, and three children, in Clashmore, Assynt, Sutherland, 1774. [SA#75]

MATHIESON, ANGUS, with his wife, and four children, in Culkein Achnacarnan, Assynt, Sutherland, 1774. [SA#78]

MATHIESON, DONALD, with his wife, one child, and one servant, in Nedd, Assynt, Sutherland, 1774. [SA#85]

MATHIESON, HUGH, wife, two children, and a servant, in Little Badidarroch, Assynt, Sutherland, 1774. [SA#73]

MATHIESON, MALCOLM, with his wife and four children, in Ardvar, Assynt, Sutherland, 1774. [SA#72]

MATHIESON, WILLIAM, with his wife, and six children, in Stoer, Assynt, Sutherland, 1774. [SA#86]

MATHIESON, ..., at Killdany, 1780. [NAS.E746.81]

MILLER, ALEXANDER, a cottar in Gills, Mey, Caithness, 1771. [NAS.GD96.679.14]

MILLER, ANDREW, soldier of Captain Alexander Mackenzie's Independent Company, 1746. [TGSI.LIII.382]

MILLER, ANDREW, a merchant and cottar in Gills, Mey, Caithness, 1771. [NAS.GD96.679.14]

MILLER, GEORGE, Treasurer of Tain, Easter Ross, 1766. [OR#408]

MILLER, GEORGE, a cottar in Mey, Caithness, 1771. [NAS.GD96.679.14]

MILLER, JAMES, a cottar in Mey, Caithness, 1771. [NAS.GD96.679.14]

MILLS, ROBERT, sailor or fisherman settled at New Tarbat, Easter Ross, 1765. [NAS.E746.80]

MITCHELL, ANDREW, sailor or fisherman settled at New Tarbat, Easter Ross, 1765. [NAS.E746.80]

MONRO, ALEXANDER, soldier of Captain Hugh McKay's Independent Company, discharged at Aviemore by Lord Loudoun in 1746. [TGSI.LIII.390]

MONRO, GEORGE, of Culcairn, Captain of an Independent Company commanded by the Earl of Loudoun at Dornoch, Sutherland, 10 March 1746. [MCP.V.31]

MONRO, GEORGE, sergeant of Captain Hugh McKay's Independent Company, died in 1746. [TGSI.LIII.389]

MONRO, Sir HARRY, of Foulis, Captain of the Earl of Loudoun's Regiment at Dornoch, Sutherland, 10 March 1746. [MCP.V.30]

MONRO, HECTOR, a tenant in Cruick, Halladale, Caithness, 1756. [NAS.GD87.SEC2.13]

MONRO, HUGH, a merchant in Clayside, 1720. [NAS.GD96.699]

MONRO, JOHN, minister of Rogart, Sutherland, from 1725 to 1753, died on 3 February 1753, husband of Elizabeth Monro, parents of three children. [F.7.98]

MONRO, JOHN, in Mason, soldier of Captain Hugh McKay's Independent Company, 17 June 1746. [TGSI.LIII.391]

MONRO, JOHN, in Strath, soldier of Captain Hugh McKay's Independent Company, 17 June 1746. [TGSI.LIII.391]

MONRO, JOHN, in Culcairn, a soldier of Captain Hugh McKay's Independent Company in 1746. [TGSI.LIII.391]

MONTGOMERIE, CHARLES, soldier of Captain Hugh McKay's Independent Company, 17 June 1746. [TGSI.LIII.390]

MONTGOMERY, JOHN, linen manufacturer in Milton of New Tarbat, Easter Ross, 1770s. [NAS.E746.94/137]

MONTGOMERY, JOHN, at Milntoun, 1780. [NAS.E746.81]

MORE, FINLAY MACFINLAY, in Tain, Easter Ross, 1766. [OR#409]

MORGAN, ALEXANDER, a soldier of Captain Hugh McKay's Independent Company in 1746. [TGSI.LIII.391]

MORRISON, ALEXANDER, in Culkin Drumbeg, Assynt, Sutherland, 1774. [SA#79]

MORRISON, ALEXANDER, with his wife, four children, and one servant, in Drumbeg, Assynt, Sutherland, 1774. [SA#79]

MORRISON, ANGUS, soldier of Captain George Mackay's Independent Company at Shiromore, 1746. [TGSI.LIII.371]

MORRISON, ANGUS, with his brother and sister, in Culkin Drumbeg, Assynt, Sutherland, 1774. [SA#79]

MORRISON, DONALD, soldier of Captain George Mackay's Independent Company at Shiromore, 1746. [TGSI.LIII.371]

MORRISON, DONALD, with his wife, and four children, in Ardvar, Assynt, Sutherland, 1774. [SA#73]

MORRISON, HECTOR, in Tarbet, soldier of Captain Hugh McKay's Independent Company, 17 June 1746. [TGSI.LIII.390]

MORRISON, HUGH, in Kylestrome, Sutherland, soldier of Captain Hugh McKay's Independent Company, 17 June 1746. [TGSI.LIII.390]

MORRISON, HUGH, in Gisgill, a soldier of Captain Hugh McKay's Independent Company in 1746. [TGSI.LIII.391]

MORRISON, HUGH, soldier of Captain George Mackay's Independent Company at Shiromore, 1746. [TGSI.LIII.371]

MORRISON, JOHN, in Glenelg, a soldier in Captain Hugh McLeod of Geanies Independent Company on 17 June 1746. [TGSI.LIII.381]

MORRISON, JOHN, son of John Morrison of Bragar, minister of Urray and Tarradale, Ross and Cromarty, from 1717 to1747, died 1 July 1747. Husband of (1) Mary, daughter of John Mackenzie of Gruinard and Christian Mackenzie, parents of Norman, and John; (2) Christian, daughter of Alexander Munro of Kilchoan, parents of Alexander and Christina. [F.7.50]

MORRISON, JOHN, with his wife, one child, and one servant, in Culkin Drumbeg, Assynt, Sutherland, 1774. [SA#79]

MORRISON, NEIL, soldier of Captain George Mackay's Independent Company at Shiromore, dead by 1746. [TGSI.LIII.371]

MORRISON, NIEL, soldier of Captain, Hugh McKay's Independent Company, 17 June 1746. [TGSI.LIII.390]

MORRISON, PATRICK, the younger, soldier of Captain Hugh McKay's Independent Company, 17 June 1746. [TGSI.LIII.390]

MORRISON, ROBERT, in Oldshoar, soldier of Captain Hugh McKay's Independent Company, 17 June 1746. [TGSI.LIII.390]

MORRISON, RORY, with his wife, and five children, in Ardvar, Assynt, Sutherland, 1774. [SA#73]

MORRISON, THOMAS, soldier of Captain George Mackay's Independent Company at Shiromore, 1746. [TGSI.LIII.371]

MORRISON, WILLIAM, corporal of Captain Hugh McKay's Independent Company in 1746. [TGSI.LIII.389]

MORRISON, WILLIAM, the elder, soldier of Captain George Mackay's Independent Company at Shiromore, 1746. [TGSI.LIII.371]

MORRISON, WILLIAM, the younger, soldier of Captain George Mackay's Independent Company at Shiromore, 1746. [TGSI.LIII.371]

MOWAT, ALEXANDER, tenant in Mey, Caithness, 1771. [NAS.GD96.679.14]

MOWAT, DONALD, a cottar in Mey, Caithness, 1771. [NAS.GD96.679.14]

MOWAT, FRANCIS, a cottar in Mey, Caithness, 1771. [NAS.GD96.679.14]

MOWAT, GEORGE, a cottar in Mey, Caithness, 1771. [NAS.GD96.679.14]

MOWAT, JAMES, tenant in Eastside of Mey, Caithness, 1771. [NAS.GD96.679.14]

MOWAT, JOHN, a cottar in Mey, Caithness, 1771. [NAS.GD96.679.14]

MOWAT, MAGNUS, tenant in Eastside of Mey, Caithness, 1771. [NAS.GD96.679.14]

MOWAT, MARY, a cottar in Gills, Mey, Caithness, 1771. [NAS.GD96.679.14]

MOWAT, PATRICK, a cottar in Mey, Caithness, 1771. [NAS.GD96.679.14]

MUNRO, ALEXANDER, in Katwall, soldier of George Munro of Culcairns' Independent Company, 1745. [TGSI.LIII.364]

MUNRO, ALEXANDER, in Nafaid in Fyrish, soldier of George Munro of Culcairns' Independent Company, 1745. [TGSI.LIII.364]

MUNRO, ALEXANDER, in Dornoch, Sutherland, soldier of Alexander Gunn's Independent Company at Shiromore, 16 June 1746. [TGSI.LIII.369]

MUNRO, ALEXANDER BAIN, in Katwall, soldier of George Munro of Culcairns' Independent Company, 1745. [TGSI.LIII.364]

MUNRO, ALEXANDER, in Alness, Easter Ross, soldier of George Munro of Culcairns' Independent Company, 1745. [TGSI.LIII.364]

MUNRO, ALEXANDER, a miller in Drummond, Easter Ross, soldier of George Munro of Culcairns' Independent Company, 1745. [TGSI.LIII.364]

MUNRO, ALEXANDER MCGILICHALLUM, in Milntown, soldier of George Munro of Culcairns' Independent Company, 1745. [TGSI.LIII.364]

MUNRO, ALEXANDER, turner in Kildermory, soldier of George Munro of Culcairns' Independent Company, 1745. [TGSI.LIII.364]

MUNRO, ALEXANDER, soldier of Captain George Mackay's Independent Company at Shiromore, 1746. [TGSI.LIII.371]

MUNRO, ALEXANDER, a tenant in Halladale, Caithness, 1756. [NAS.GD87.SEC2.13]

MUNRO, ALEXANDER, sr., a shoemaker in Tain, Easter Ross, 1766. [OR#409]

MUNRO, ALEXANDER, jr., a shoemaker in Tain, Easter Ross, 1766. [OR#409]

MUNRO, ALEXANDER, tacksman of Tain mill, Easter Ross, 1766. [OR#409]

MUNRO, ALEXANDER, tenant in Dalkinloch, 1770. [NAS.E746.167.5]

MUNRO, ALEXANDER, with his wife, in Achmelvich, Assynt, Sutherland, 1774. [SA#71]

MUNRO, ALEXANDER, with his wife, and five children, in Stoer, Assynt, Sutherland, 1774. [SA#86]

MUNRO, ANDREW, in Island Chorry, 1740. [NAS.GD84/2/23]

MUNRO, CHARLES, corporal of George Munro of Culcairns' Independent Company, 1745. [TGSI.LIII.364]

MUNRO, DANIEL, educated at Marischal College, Aberdeen, minister of Tain, Easter Ross, and Morinnis from 1745 to 1748, died 10 November 1748. Husband of Margaret Spence, parents of Anne, Andrew, James, Katherine, Robert, and John. [F.7.71]

MUNRO, DAVID, corporal of George Munro of Culcairns' Independent Company, 1745. [TGSI.LIII.364]

MUNRO, DAVID, a merchant in Tain, Easter Ross, 1766. [OR#408]

MUNRO, DAVID, a boatman in Tain, Easter Ross, 1766. [OR#409]

MUNRO, DONALD MCFINLAY ROY, in Teanich, soldier of George Munro of Culcairns' Independent Company, 1745. [TGSI.LIII.364]

MUNRO, DONALD, in Bridgend, soldier of George Munro of Culcairns' Independent Company, 1745. [TGSI.LIII.364]

MUNRO, DONALD, in Dalbreak, soldier of George Munro of Culcairns' Independent Company, 1745. [TGSI.LIII.364]

MUNRO, DONALD GRASSICH, in Kiltearn, soldier of George Munro of Culcairns' Independent Company, 1745. [TGSI.LIII.364]

MUNRO, DONALD, turner in Kildermory, soldier of George Munro of Culcairns' Independent Company, 1745. [TGSI.LIII.364]

MUNRO, DONALD, in Teanaird, soldier of George Munro of Culcairns' Independent Company, 1745. [TGSI.LIII.364]

MUNRO, DONALD, the younger, in Teanaird, soldier of George Munro of Culcairns' Independent Company, 1745. [TGSI.LIII.364]

MUNRO, DONALD MCFINLAY ROY, in Inchdown, soldier of George Munro of Culcairns' Independent Company, 1745. [TGSI.LIII.364]

MUNRO, DONALD, in Druminloy, soldier of George Munro of Culcairns' Independent Company, 1745. [TGSI.LIII.364]

MUNRO, DONALD BAIN, in Drummond, Easter Ross, soldier of George Munro of Culcairns' Independent Company, 1745. [TGSI.LIII.364]

MUNRO, DONALD MCCALLIE, in Drummond, Easter Ross, soldier of George Munro of Culcairns' Independent Company, 1745. [TGSI.LIII.364]

MUNRO, DONALD, in Katwell, soldier of George Munro of Culcairns' Independent Company, 1745. [TGSI.LIII.364]

MUNRO, DONALD BAINE, in Auchany, soldier of George Munro of Culcairns' Independent Company, 1745. [TGSI.LIII.364]

MUNRO, DONALD, in Store, a soldier in Captain Hugh McLeod of Geanies Independent Company on 17 June 1746. [TGSI.LIII.380]

MUNRO, DONALD, a sergeant in Captain Hugh McLeod of Geanies Independent Company on 17 June 1746. [TGSI.LIII.380]

MUNRO, DONALD, in Ribbigill, soldier of Captain George Mackay's Independent Company at Shiromore, dead by 1746. [TGSI.LIII.371]

MUNRO, DONALD, in Farr, soldier of Captain George Mackay's Independent Company at Shiromore, 1746. [TGSI.LIII.371]

MUNRO, DONALD, in Muckle Altas, a soldier in Captain Hugh McLeod of Geanies Independent Company on 17 June 1746. [TGSI.LIII.381]

MUNRO, DONALD, in Boath, a soldier in Captain Hugh McLeod of Geanies Independent Company on 17 June 1746. [TGSI.LIII.381]

MUNRO, FINLAY, with his wife and five children, in Ardvar, Assynt, Sutherland, 1774. [SA#72]

MUNRO, GEORGE, born in 1705 at Dunrobin, Sutherland, son of George Munro, a farmer. Minister of Farr, Sutherland, from 1754 to 1779, died 1 May 1779. Husband of Barbara Mackay, and father of Katherine and Mary. [F.7.107]

MUNRO, GEORGE MCGILLICHALLUM, in Foulis, soldier of George Munro of Culcairns' Independent Company, 1745. [TGSI.LIII.364]

MUNRO, GEORGE, in Obsdale, soldier of George Munro of Culcairns' Independent Company, 1745. [TGSI.LIII.364]

MUNRO, GEORGE, in Newtown, soldier of George Munro of Culcairns' Independent Company, 1745. [TGSI.LIII.364]

MUNRO, GEORGE, in Auchany, soldier of George Munro of Culcairns' Independent Company, 1745. [TGSI.LIII.364]

MUNRO, GEORGE, in Torvirie, soldier of Alexander Gunn's Independent Company at Shiromore, 16 June 1746. [TGSI.LIII.369]

MUNRO, Sir HARRY, of Foulis, Chamberlain of Ross, 1753. [NAS.E746.29]

MUNRO, HARRY, a merchant in Tain, Easter Ross, 1766. [OR#408]

MUNRO, HECTOR OIG, in Bognahavine, soldier of George Munro of Culcairns' Independent Company, 1745. [TGSI.LIII.364]

MUNRO, HUGH, son of Andrew Munro of Teanaird, educated at St Andrews, minister of Tain, Easter Ross, and Morinnis from 1701 to 1744. Husband of (1) Jean Thomson, parents of Jean; (2) Jean Ross, parents of Alexander, Robert, Christina, Mary, John (1), John (2), Anna, Andrew, Hugh, Margaret, Janet, and Duncan. [F.7.71]

MUNRO, HUGH, the younger of Achany, Ensign of the Munro Independent Company, at Inverness 1745. [MCP.92]

MUNRO, HUGH, sergeant of George Munro of Culcairns' Independent Company, 1745. [TGSI.LIII.364]

MUNRO, HUGH, of Ardulie, sergeant of George Munro of Culcairns' Independent Company, 1745. [TGSI.LIII.364]

MUNRO, HUGH CALLANACH, in Foulis, soldier of George Munro of Culcairns' Independent Company, 1745. [TGSI.LIII.365]

MUNRO, HUGH, in Kydoich, soldier of George Munro of Culcairns' Independent Company, 1745. [TGSI.LIII.365]

MUNRO, HUGH, in Auchnacullan, soldier of George Munro of Culcairns' Independent Company, 1745. [TGSI.LIII.365]

MUNRO, HUGH, soldier of Captain George Mackay's Independent Company at Shiromore, 1746. [TGSI.LIII.371]

MUNRO, HUGH, of Teaninich, 1748. [NAS.E746.1]

MUNRO, HUGH, a silversmith in Tain, Easter Ross, 1766. [OR#408]

MUNRO, JAMES, in Tain, Easter Ross, 1766. [OR#409]

MUNRO, JOHN, born 1708 in Uist, son of Captain Robert Munro of Erribol and Christian Fraser, graduated MA from King's College, Aberdeen, 1728, minister of Eddrachillis, Sutherland, from 1744 to 1755, died 13 February 1755. Husband of Christian MacLeod, and father of Katherine, George, Robert, Alexander, Mary, Hugh, Christian, and Robert. [F.7.104]

MUNRO, JOHN, son of Robert Munro. Minister of Halkirk, Caithness, 1706 to 1743, died 18 April 1743. Husband of Janet Gun, father of John, George, Henry, Robert, David, and Janet. [F.7.122]

MUNRO, JOHN MCFARQUHAR, in Wester Foulis, soldier of George Munro of Culcairns' Independent Company, 1745. [TGSI.LIII.365]

MUNRO, JOHN BALLACH, in Culcairn, soldier of George Munro of Culcairns' Independent Company, 1745. [TGSI.LIII.365]

MUNRO, JOHN BAIN, in Balblair, soldier of George Munro of Culcairns' Independent Company, 1745. [TGSI.LIII.365]

MUNRO, JOHN NAFFAID, in Teanriven, soldier of George Munro of Culcairns' Independent Company, 1745. [TGSI.LIII.365]

MUNRO, JOHN MCGILLISPICK, soldier of George Munro of Culcairns' Independent Company, 1745. [TGSI.LIII.365]

MUNRO, JOHN ALLANSON, in Newtown, soldier of George Munro of Culcairns' Independent Company, 1745. [TGSI.LIII.365]

MUNRO, JOHN, in Dornoch, soldier of Alexander Gunn's Independent Company at Shiromore, 16 June 1746. [TGSI.LIII.369]

MUNRO, JOHN, in Muckle Altas, a soldier in Captain Hugh McLeod of Geanies Independent Company on 17 June 1746. [TGSI.LIII.381]

MUNRO, JOHN, a sergeant in Captain Hugh McLeod of Geanies Independent Company on 17 June 1746. [TGSI.LIII.380]

MUNRO, JOHN, in Layne, a soldier in Captain Hugh McLeod of Geanies Independent Company on 17 June 1746. [TGSI.LIII.380]

MUNRO, JOHN, a widower, with six children, and a servant in Balchladich, Assynt, Sutherland, 1774. [SA#74]

MUNRO, JOHN, in Clashnessie, Assynt, Sutherland, 1774. [SA#76]

MUNRO, JOHN, with his wife and two children, in Oldeny, Assynt, Sutherland, 1774. [SA#85]

MUNRO, JOHN, with his wife, one child and two servants, in Stoer, Assynt, Sutherland, 1774. [SA#86]

MUNRO, JOSEPH, born 1714, son of Reverend Robert Munro in Kincardine, Easter Ross, educated at St Andrews, minister of Edderton, Easter Ross, from 1742 to 1785, died 16 March 1785. Husband of Barbara Ross, parents of Annabella, Walter, Elizabeth, Robert, Joseph, Janet, Helen, Barbara, and Matthew. [F.7.54]

MUNRO, KATHRINE, with one servant in Ledbeg, Assynt, Sutherland, 1774. [SA#83]

MUNRO, MARY, died 29 March 1744, wife of Donald Ross tacksman of Invershin. [Kincardine gravestone, Wester Ross]

MUNRO, NEIL, with his wife, in Achmelvich, Assynt, Sutherland, 1774. [SA#71]

MUNRO, NIEL BALLACH, in Wester Foulis, soldier of George Munro of Culcairns' Independent Company, 1745. [TGSI.LIII.365]

MUNRO, ROBERT, third son of George Munro, educated at St Andrews, minister of Kincardine, presbytery of Tain, Easter Ross, from 1711 to 1741, died 10 February 1741. Husband of Janet Pirrie, parents of Joseph and William. [F.7.60]

MUNRO, ROBERT, born 1720 son of John Munro minister of Suddie, Ross and Cromarty. Minister of Knockbain, Ross and Cromarty, from 1747 to 1790, died 27 September 1790. Husband of (1) Isobel, daughter of Colin Graham of Drynie, parents of Burnet, (2) Isobel McKenzie; (3) Seymour Munro. [F.7.15]

MUNRO, ROBERT, sergeant of George Munro of Culcairns' Independent Company, 1745. [TGSI.LIII.364]

MUNRO, ROBERT MACANGUS, in Katwall, soldier of George Munro of Culcairns' Independent Company, 1745. [TGSI.LIII.365]

MUNRO, ROBERT BAINE, in Newton, soldier of George Munro of Culcairns' Independent Company, 1745. [TGSI.LIII.365]

MUNRO, ROBERT, in Rufarqr, soldier of George Munro of Culcairns' Independent Company, 1745. [TGSI.LIII.365]

MUNRO, ROBERT, surgeon in Wester Foulis, soldier of George Munro of Culcairns' Independent Company, 1745. [TGSI.LIII.365]

MUNRO, RODERICK, in Culcraigie, soldier of George Munro of Culcairns' Independent Company, 1745. [TGSI.LIII.365]

MUNRO, RONALD, in Swardell, soldier of George Munro of Culcairns' Independent Company, 1745. [TGSI.LIII.365]

MUNRO, RORIE, in Tain, Easter Ross, 1766. [OR#409]

MUNRO, WILLIAM, the elder, in Obsdale, soldier of George Munro of Culcairns' Independent Company, 1745. [TGSI.LIII.365]

MUNRO, WILLIAM, the younger, in Obsdale, soldier of George Munro of Culcairns' Independent Company, 1745. [TGSI.LIII.365]

MUNRO, WILLIAM MCVRIKAN, in Teanriven, soldier of George Munro of Culcairns' Independent Company, 1745. [TGSI.LIII.365]

MUNRO, WILLIAM, in Balchastle, soldier of George Munro of Culcairns' Independent Company, 1745. [TGSI.LIII.365]

MUNRO, WILLIAM, miller in Mulinuoran, soldier of George Munro of Culcairns' Independent Company, 1745. [TGSI.LIII.365]

MUNRO, WILLIAM MCGILICHALLUM, in Balcony, soldier of George Munro of Culcairns' Independent Company, 1745. [TGSI.LIII.365]

MUNRO. WILLIAM BUY, in Contrilich, soldier of George Munro of Culcairns' Independent Company, 1745. [TGSI.LIII.365]

MUNRO, WILLIAM, in Drummond, Easter Ross, soldier of George Munro of Culcairns' Independent Company, 1745. [TGSI.LIII.365]

MUNRO, WILLIAM, in Plaids, soldier of George Munro of Culcairns' Independent Company, 1745. [TGSI.LIII.365]

MUNRO, WILLIAM, in Altas, a soldier in Captain Hugh McLeod of Geanies Independent Company on 17 June 1746. [TGSI.LIII.380]

MUNRO, WILLIAM, soldier of Captain George Mackay's Independent Company at Shiromore, 1746. [TGSI.LIII.371]

MUNRO, WILLIAM, in Skudchaill, a soldier of the Master of Ross' Independent Company at Linachan, 14 June 1746. [TGSI.LIII.392]

MUNRO, WILLIAM, in Morangie, a soldier of the Master of Ross' Independent Company at Linachan, 14 June 1746. [TGSI.LIII.392]

MUNRO, WILLIAM, born 1747, gardener at Rosehall, died 10 June 1821. [Auchness gravestone, Sutherland]

MURCHISON, ALEXANDER, soldier of Captain Alexander Mackenzie's Independent Company, 1746. [TGSI.LIII.382]

MURCHISON, DAVID, corporal of Captain Alexander Mackenzie's Independent Company, 1746. [TGSI.LIII.382]

MURCHISON, DONALD, soldier of Captain Alexander Mackenzie's Independent Company, 1746. [TGSI.LIII.383]

MURCHISON, EVANDER, soldier of Captain Alexander Mackenzie's Independent Company, 1746. [TGSI.LIII.382]

MURCHISON, JOHN, in Coish, soldier of Captain Alexander Mackenzie's Independent Company, 1746. [TGSI.LIII.382]

MURCHISON, JOHN, corporal of Captain Colin Mackenzie's Independent Company, 1746. [TGSI.LIII.384]

MURCHISON, KATHARINE, in Toskaig, Applecross, Wester Ross, 1718. [TGSI.LIV.452]

MURCHISON, MURDO, in Coish, soldier of Captain Alexander Mackenzie's Independent Company, deserted in 1746. [TGSI.LIII.382]

MURCHISON, MURDO, in Lochalse, soldier of Captain Alexander Mackenzie's Independent Company, 1746. [TGSI.LIII.383]

MURCHISON, WILLIAM, soldier of Captain Alexander Mackenzie's Independent Company, 1746. [TGSI.LIII.382]

MURCHISON, WILLIAM, in Achterteir, soldier of Captain Alexander Mackenzie's Independent Company, 1746. [TGSI.LIII.382]

MURCHY, CHRISTOPHER, in Barradale, Applecross, Wester Ross, 1718. [TGSI.LIV.451]

MURRAY, ALEXANDER, a violer and glover in Tain, Easter Ross, 1766. [OR#408]

MURRAY, DAVID, in Edertown, a soldier of the Master of Ross' Independent Company at Linachan, 14 June 1746. [TGSI.LIII.391]

MURRAY, DONALD, a cottar in Mey, Caithness, 1771. [NAS.GD96.679.14]

MURRAY, FRANCIS, sailor or fisherman settled at New Tarbat, Easter Ross, 1765. [NAS.E746.80]

MURRAY, JOHN, in Auchvandra, soldier of Alexander Gunn's Independent Company at Shiromore, 16 June 1746. [TGSI.LIII.369]

MURRAY, WILLIAM, soldier of Captain George Mackay's Independent Company at Shiromore, 1746. [TGSI.LIII.371]

NICOLSON, ALEXANDER, born 1724 son of Patrick Nicolson in Kiltarlity. Minister of Thurso, Caithness, from 1752 to 1785, died on 28 August 1785. Husband of (1) Mary Dunbar, (2) Mary Honyman, and father of Margaret, Patrick, James, and Janet. [F.7.137]

NICOLSON, ALEXANDER, soldier of Captain Alexander Mackenzie's Independent Company, dead by 1746. [TGSI.LIII.383]

NICOLSON, JAMES, born 13 April 1739 son of Patrick Nicolson minister of Kiltarlity. Minister of Durinish from 1762 to 1766, then of Halkirk, Caithness, from 1766 to 1768, drowned on 25 September 1768. [F.7.122]

NICOLSON, or MCNICOL, JOHN, with his wife, one child, and two servants, in Achnacarnan, Assynt, Sutherland, 1774. [SA#72]

NICOLSON, JOHN, in Clashnessie, Assynt, Sutherland, 1774. [SA#76]

NICOLSON, or MCNICOL, NEIL, with his wife and five children, in Achnacarnan, Assynt, Sutherland, 1774. [SA#72]

NIENALISTER, MARY, in Rishell, Applecross, Wester Ross, 1718. [TGSI.LIV.450]

OIG, JOHN, in Tain, Easter Ross, 1766. [OR#409]

OIG, THOMAS, a musician in Tain, Easter Ross, 1766. [OR#408]

OLIPHANT, ALEXANDER, born 1710 son of James Oliphant in Wick, Caithness. Minister of Bower, Caithness, from 1739 to 1779, died 2 November 1779. Husband of Margaret Brodie, and father of Katherine, Marjory, James, John, Katherine, Elizabeth, George (died in Grenada 1773), Mary, and Anna. [F.7.115]

OSWALD, JAMES, son of Reverend George Oswald and Margaret Murray. Minister of Dunnet, Caithness, from 1726 to 1750. [F.7.120]

POLSON, JOHN, tenant in Eastside of Mey, Caithness, 1771. [NAS.GD96.679.14]

POPE, ALEXANDER, born 1706 son of Hector Pope. Schoolmaster of Reay, Caithness, 1725, then minister there from 1734 1778, died 2 March 1782. Husband of (1) Margaret Sutherland, (2) Janet Ross, and father of William, Alexander, Harry, Abigail, Thomas, John, James, and Charles. [F.7.133]

PORTEOUS, JOHN, born 1704 in Inverness, educated at King's College, Aberdeen, minister of Kilmuir Easter, Ross and Cromarty, from 1734 to 1775, died 7 January 1775. Husband of Jane Innes. [F.7.58]

RAE, DONALD, a wright in Tain, Easter Ross, 1766. [OR#408]

RAINY, GEORGE, born 1734 son of John Rennie a farmer in Turriff, Aberdeenshire, educated at Aberdeen University, minister of Creich, Sutherland, from 1771 to 1810, died on 23 October 1810, husband of Ann Robertson, parents of several children including Gilbert (1782-1808) who died in Demerara, and George (1790-1863) a merchant in Demerara. [F.7.82]

REAH, JOHN, soldier of Captain Alexander Mackenzie's Independent Company, dead by 1746. [TGSI.LIII.382]

REED, DONALD, a boatman in Tain, Easter Ross, 1766.
[OR#409]

REICH, JOHN, in Little Oassie, soldier of Captain Colin Mackenzie's Independent Company, 1746.
[TGSI.LIII.385]

REICH, WILLIAM, in Little Oassie, soldier of Captain Colin Mackenzie's Independent Company, 1746.
[TGSI.LIII.385]

REID, ALEXANDER, master of the Helen and Margaret of Cromarty, 1748. [NAS.E504.17.1]

REID, ALEXANDER, a wigmaker in Tain, Easter Ross, 1766.
[OR#408]

REID, ALEXANDER, a wright in Tain, Easter Ross, 1766.
[OR#408]

REID, JOHN, master of the Adventure of Cromarty arrived in Inverness on 10 September 1763 from Cadiz, Spain.
[NAS.E504.17.3]

REID, JOHN, baillie of Tain, Easter Ross 1766. [OR#408]

REID, JOHN, a wigmaker in Tain, Easter Ross, 1766.
[OR#408]

REID, JOHN, a wright in Tain, Easter Ross, 1766. [OR#408]

RICHARDSON, JAMES, an Excise officer in Wick, Caithness, 1753. [NAS.B73.2/1/12-13]

RIOCH, DONALD, tacksman of Urray, Ross and Cromarty, 1773. [NAS.GD46.SEC.1/212]

ROBERTSON, ANDREW, son of Hugh Robertson in Balconie, minister of Farr, Sutherland, 1727 to 1731, minister of Kiltearn and Lemlair from 1731 to 1769, died 6 July 1769. Husband of Mary Oswald, parents of Mary, Harry, and Margaret. [F.7.43, 106]

ROBERTSON, DAVID, master of the Hercules of Inverness, 1744. [NAS.E504.17.1]

ROBERTSON, DONALD, with his wife, two children, and one servant, in Glenlerag, Assynt, Sutherland, 1774. [SA#80]

ROBERTSON, DONALD, master of the Isobel of Wick, Caithness, arrived in Inverness on 25 December 1772 from Leith. [NAS.E504.17.4[

ROBERTSON, FRANCIS, son of Francis Robertson and his wife Helen Ross in Balcony. Graduated MA from St Andrews in 1710, schoolmaster of Tain, Easter Ross, ordained as minister of the parish of Clyne, Sutherland, in 1719, died 14 May 1763. He married Jane Sutherland in January 1723, and they were the parents of Francis died in England 1749, Gilbert born 1727, Charles died 1752, James born 1733, died 1749, Margaret born 1738, Mary born 1740, Janet born 1742, Jean born 1744, and Henrietta born 1748. [F.7.80]

ROBERTSON, FRANCIS, master of the Elizabeth of Cromarty, arrived in Inverness on 22 October 1767 from Kirkcaldy. [NAS.E504.17.4]

ROBERTSON, GILBERT, born 1702 son of George Robertson a farmer in Balconie, Kiltearn, minister of Kincardine, presbytery of Tain, Easter Ross, from 1742 to 1774, died 17 March 1774. Husband of Christian Bayne, parents of Harry, Anne, John (died in Tobago), and George (died in Demerara). [F.7.61]

ROBERTSON, GILBERT, a merchant in Tain, Easter Ross, 1766. [OR#408]

ROBERTSON, HARRY, MA, minister of Clyne, Sutherland, from 1771 to 1776. [F.7.80]

ROBERTSON, JAMES, minister at Lochbroom, Wester Ross, 1757-1774. [NAS.E746.82]

ROBERTSON, JOHN, born 1706, educated at St Andrews, minister of Killearnan, Ross and Cromarty, from 1731 to 1743, died 25 February 1743. Husband of Katherine, daughter of Thomas Chisholm minister of Kilmorack. [F.7.12]

ROBERTSON, KENNETH, tacksman of Rosemarkie, the Black Isle, 1774. [NAS.GD46.SEC.1/212]

ROBERTSON, ROBERT, born 1692 son of Colin Robertson of Kindeace and Rebecca Munro, educated at Edinburgh University, minister of Loth, Sutherland, from 1721 to 1730,minister of Edderton from 1730 to 1740, died 18 December 1740. [F.7.53/95]

ROBERTSON, WILLIAM, master of the Mercury of Tain, , arrived in Inverensss during October 1760 from St Lucar, Spain, and arrived in Inverness during November 1760 from Christiansand, Norway; master of the Isobel of Wick, Caithness, arrived in Inverness on 21 September 1774 from Newcastle, England. [NAS.E504.17.3/4]

RORY, DONALD, in Corvick, soldier of Captain Colin Mackenzie's Independent Company, 1746. [TGSI.LIII.385]

ROSE, ADAM, born 1713, educated at King's College, Aberdeen, minister of Dingwall, Ross and Cromarty, from 1743 to 1780, died 21 March 1780. Husband of Isobel Beton, parents of Grissel, Janet, Daniel, Adam, Isabel, and Margaret. [F.7.34]

ROSE, HUGH, son of Hugh Rose of Clava, sasine of lands in Nairn dated 14 April 1729. [SCA.FL5/11]

ROSE, HUGH, born in Easter Ross 1730, educated at St Andrews, schoolmaster in Invergordon, minister in Creich 1759 to 1770; minister in Tain, Easter Ross, and Morinnis from 1770 to 1774, died 23 September 1774. Husband of Mary McCulloch, parents of George, David, James, Roderick, Hugh [sometime in the West Indies], Christian, and William. [F.7.72/82]

ROSE, ROBERT, a silversmith in Tain, Easter Ross, 1766. [OR#408]

ROSE, WILLIAM, minister at Kildonan, Sutherland, 1725 to 1739, at Loth from 1739 to1755, died on 12 February 1755, husband of Jean Anderson, parents of five children. [F.7.96]

ROSIE, JOHN, a cottar in Mey, Caithness, 1771. [NAS.GD96.679.14]

ROSIE, WILLIAM, tenant in Mey, Caithness, 1771. [NAS.GD96.679.14]

ROSIE, WILLIAM, tenant in Eastside of Mey, Caithness, 1771. [NAS.GD96.679.14]

ROSIE, WILLIAM, a cottar in Gills, Mey, Caithness, 1771. [NAS.GD96.679.14]

ROSS, ALEXANDER, a merchant in Tain, Easter Ross, husband of Catherine Fraser, purchased lands in Dornoch in 1712. [SCA.FL5/8]

ROSS, ALEXANDER, in Evelacks, soldier of Alexander Gunn's Independent Company at Shiromore, 16 June 1746. [TGSI.LIII.369]

ROSS, ALEXANDER, in Ardgy, a soldier of the Master of Ross' Independent Company at Linachan, 14 June 1746. [TGSI.LIII.391]

ROSS, ALEXANDER, in Langll, a soldier of the Master of Ross' Independent Company at Linachan, 14 June 1746. [TGSI.LIII.392]

ROSS, ALEXANDER, was served as heir to his father Malcolm Ross of Pitcalnie, parish of Nigg, Ross-shire, who died in April 1734, on 12 April 1750. [NAS.SH]

ROSS, ALEXANDER, a merchant in Tain, Easter Ross, 1766. [OR#408]

ROSS, ALEXANDER, a shoemaker in Tain, Easter Ross, 1766. [OR#409]

ROSS, ALEXANDER, in Strathrustle, Tain, Easter Ross, 1766. [OR#409]

ROSS, ALEXANDER, in Aldiewillen, a soldier of the Master of Ross' Independent Company at Linachan, 14 June 1746. [TGSI.LIII.391]

ROSS, ALEXANDER, in Aldanfin, a soldier of the Master of Ross' Independent Company at Linachan, 14 June 1746. [TGSI.LIII.392]

ROSS, ALEXANDER DOW SMALL, a soldier of the Master of Ross' Independent Company at Linachan, 14 June 1746. [TGSI.LIII.392]

ROSS, ALEXANDER, in Kincardine, a soldier of the Master of Ross' Independent Company at Linachan, 14 June 1746. [TGSI.LIII.392]

ROSS, ALEXANDER, in Aldanguich, a soldier of the Master of Ross' Independent Company at Linachan, 14 June 1746. [TGSI.LIII.392]

ROSS, ALEXANDER, in Keanlochin, a soldier of the Master of Ross' Independent Company at Linachan, 14 June 1746. [TGSI.LIII.392]

ROSS, ALL., in Old Town, a soldier of the Master of Ross' Independent Company at Linachan, 14 June 1746. [TGSI.LIII.391]

ROSS, ALL., in Lubcoinich, a soldier of the Master of Ross' Independent Company at Linachan, 14 June 1746. [TGSI.LIII.392]

ROSS, ALL. MCEAN, in Aldanfim, a soldier of the Master of Ross' Independent Company at Linachan, 14 June 1746. [TGSI.LIII.392]

ROSS, ANDREW, in the Hill of Tain, Easter Ross, 1766.
[OR#409]

ROSS, ANGUS, in Hack, a soldier of the Master of Ross'
Independent Company at Linachan, 14 June 1746.
[TGSI.LIII.392]

ROSS, ANGUS, a merchant in Tain, Easter Ross, 1766.
[OR#408]

ROSS, DANIEL ROY, in Kindease, a soldier of the Master of
Ross' Independent Company at Linachan, 14 June 1746.
[TGSI.LIII.392]

ROSS, DAVID, born 1673, son of Reverend George Ross in
Kincardine, educated at St Andrews, schoolmaster of
Tain, , minister of Tarbat, Easter Ross, from 1707 to
1748, died 18 October 1748. Husband of Margaret Ross.
[F.7.75]

ROSS, DAVID, in Springidell, soldier of Alexander Gunn's
Independent Company at Shiromore, 16 June 1746.
[TGSI.LIII.369]

ROSS, DAVID, in Kanrive, a soldier in Captain Hugh McLeod
of Geanies Independent Company on 17 June 1746.
[TGSI.LIII.381]

ROSS, DAVID, born 1711, educated at Marischal College,
Aberdeen, schoolmaster at Nigg and Tarbat, Easter Ross,
minister of Kincardine, presbytery of Tain, Easter Ross,
1742, died 11 May 1742. [F.7.61]

ROSS, DAVID, in Strathrustle, a soldier in Captain Hugh
McLeod of Geanies Independent Company on 17 June
1746. [TGSI.LIII.380]

ROSS, DAVID, a corporal of the Master of Ross' Independent
Company at Linachan, 14 June 1746. [TGSI.LIII.391]

ROSS, DAVID, in Drumavaich, a soldier of the Master of
Ross' Independent Company at Linachan, 14 June 1746.
[TGSI.LIII.391]

ROSS, DAVID, in Dalchuill, a soldier of the Master of Ross' Independent Company at Linachan, 14 June 1746. [TGSI.LIII.392]

ROSS, DAVID, in Glenmore, a soldier of the Master of Ross' Independent Company at Linachan, 14 June 1746. [TGSI.LIII.392]

ROSS, DAVID DOW, in Tain, Easter Ross, a soldier of the Master of Ross' Independent Company at Linachan, 14 June 1746. [TGSI.LIII.392]

ROSS, DAVID, soldier of Captain George Mackay's Independent Company at Shiromore, 1746. [TGSI.LIII.371]

ROSS, DAVID, formerly a soldier in a Highland Independent Company, then tacksman of Drimvaich, 1756. [NAS.E746.113.6/1]

ROSS, DAVID, of Inverchasley, Provost of Tain, Easter Ross, 1766. [OR#408]

ROSS, DAVID, baillie of Tain, Easter Ross, 1766. [OR#408]

ROSS, DAVID, sr. a merchant in Tain, Easter Ross, 1766. [OR#408]

ROSS, DAVID, jr., a merchant in Tain, Easter Ross, 1766. [OR#408]

ROSS, DAVID, a dyer in Tain, Easter Ross, 1766. [OR#409]

ROSS, DAVID, miller at the Mill of Sronchubie, Assynt, Sutherland, with his wife, and three children, 1774. [SA#87]

ROSS, DONALD, in Newmore, soldier of George Munro of Culcairns' Independent Company, 1745. [TGSI.LIII.365]

ROSS, DONALD, shoemaker in Fyrish, soldier of George Munro of Culcairns' Independent Company, 1745. [TGSI.LIII.365]

ROSS, DONALD, in Despolie, soldier of Captain Hugh McKay's Independent Company, 17 June 1746. [TGSI.LIII.390]

ROSS, DONALD, in Greeny, a soldier of the Master of Ross' Independent Company at Linachan, 14 June 1746. [TGSI.LIII.391]

ROSS, DONALD GRUH, in Glencalvie, a soldier of the Master of Ross' Independent Company at Linachan, 14 June 1746. [TGSI.LIII.392]

ROSS, DONALD, in Cambuscurry, a soldier of the Master of Ross' Independent Company at Linachan, 14 June 1746. [TGSI.LIII.391]

ROSS, DONALD, in "Mcpt East", a corporal of the Master of Ross' Independent Company at Linachan, 14 June 1746. [TGSI.LIII.391]

ROSS, DONALD, in Rarrichies, a soldier of the Master of Ross' Independent Company at Linachan, 14 June 1746. [TGSI.LIII.392]

ROSS, DONALD, in Kenich, Glencalvy, a soldier of the Master of Ross' Independent Company at Linachan, 14 June 1746. [TGSI.LIII.392]

ROSS, DONALD, born 1692, minister of Fearn, Ross and Cromarty, from 1742 to 1770, died 2 September 1775. Husband of Elizabeth Ross, parents of Ann. [F.7.56]

ROSS, DONALD MCEAN VIG, a soldier in Captain Hugh McLeod of Geanies Independent Company on 17 June 1746. [TGSI.LIII.381]

ROSS, DONALD, in Leters, a soldier of the Master of Ross' Independent Company at Linachan, 14 June 1746. [TGSI.LIII.391]

ROSS, DONALD, a periwigmaker, a soldier of the Master of Ross' Independent Company at Linachan, 14 June 1746. [TGSI.LIII.392]

ROSS, DONALD, soldier of Captain George Mackay's Independent Company at Shiromore, 1746. [TGSI.LIII.371]

ROSS, DONALD, in Keanlochin, a soldier of the Master of Ross' Independent Company at Linachan, 14 June 1746. [TGSI.LIII.392]

ROSS, DONALD, a merchant in Tain, Easter Ross, 1766 [OR#408]

ROSS, DONALD, a silversmith in Tain, Easter Ross, 1766. [OR#408]

ROSS, DONALD, a tailor in Tain, Easter Ross, 1766. [OR#408]

ROSS, DONALD, fish merchant in Lochinver, Assynt, Sutherland, 1776. [NAS.E746.129]

ROSS, DUNCAN, was served as heir to his father David Ross of Kindeace on 12 June 1751. [NAS.SH; GD87.Sec.2/12]

ROSS, GEORGE, sergeant of George Munro of Culcairns' Independent Company, 1745. [TGSI.LIII.364]

ROSS, HECTOR, in Ballichraggan, soldier of George Munro of Culcairns' Independent Company, 1745. [TGSI.LIII.365]

ROSS, HECTOR, a sergeant of the Master of Ross' Independent Company at Linachan, 14 June 1746. [TGSI.LIII.391]

ROSS, HECTOR, in Croick, a soldier of the Master of Ross' Independent Company at Linachan, 14 June 1746. [TGSI.LIII.391]

ROSS, HECTOR, soldier of Captain George Mackay's Independent Company at Shiromore, 1746. [TGSI.LIII.371]

ROSS, HUGH, in Leters, a soldier of the Master of Ross' Independent Company at Linachan, 14 June 1746. [TGSI.LIII.391]

ROSS, HUGH, in Tulimtarvie, a soldier of the Master of Ross' Independent Company at Linachan, 14 June 1746. [TGSI.LIII.391]

ROSS, HUGH, in Dibidill, a soldier of the Master of Ross' Independent Company at Linachan, 14 June 1746. [TGSI.LIII.391]

ROSS, HUGH, in Glencalvie, a soldier of the Master of Ross' Independent Company at Linachan, 14 June 1746. [TGSI.LIII.392]

ROSS, HUGH, born 1720 son of John Ross overseer at Craigroy, Edderton, Easter Ross, graduated MA from Marischal College in 1736, minister of Kildonan, Sutherland, from 1755 to 1761, died on 2 February 1761, husband of Ann Houston, and parents of Elizabeth Kerr Ross. [F.7.90]

ROSS, HUGH, a baillie of Tain, Easter Ross, 1766. [OR#408]

ROSS, HUGH, a pewterer in Tain, Easter Ross, 1766. [OR#408]

ROSS, HUGH, in Narrein, Tain, Easter Ross, 1766. [OR#409]

ROSS, JAMES OAG, in Alness, Easter Ross, soldier of George Munro of Culcairns' Independent Company, 1745. [TGSI.LIII.365]

ROSS, JAMES, a shoemaker in Tain, Easter Ross, 1766. [OR#409]

ROSS, JOHN MCGILLICHALLUM, in Newtown, soldier of George Munro of Culcairns' Independent Company, 1745. [TGSI.LIII.365]

ROSS, JOHN, in Achness, a soldier in Captain Hugh McLeod of Geanies Independent Company on 17 June 1746. [TGSI.LIII.380]

ROSS, JOHN, in Tayler Douny, a soldier of the Master of Ross' Independent Company at Linachan, 14 June 1746. [TGSI.LIII.391]

ROSS, JOHN, in Glaskeill, a soldier of the Master of Ross' Independent Company at Linachan, 14 June 1746. [TGSI.LIII.392]

ROSS, or DOW, JOHN, in Glencalvie, a soldier of the Master of Ross' Independent Company at Linachan, 14 June 1746. [TGSI.LIII.391]

ROSS, JOHN, soldier of Captain George Mackay's Independent Company at Shiromore, 1746. [TGSI.LIII.371]

ROSS, JOHN, in Easterfin, a soldier of the Master of Ross' Independent Company at Linachan, 14 June 1746. [TGSI.LIII.392]

ROSS, JOHN, a sergeant of the Master of Ross' Independent Company at Linachan, 14 June 1746. [TGSI.LIII.391]

ROSS, JOHN, a corporal of the Master of Ross' Independent Company at Linachan, 14 June 1746. [TGSI.LIII.391]

ROSS, JOHN, in Arynahira, a soldier of the Master of Ross' Independent Company at Linachan, 14 June 1746. [TGSI.LIII.392]

ROSS, JOHN, in Salachy, a soldier of the Master of Ross' Independent Company at Linachan, 14 June 1746. [TGSI.LIII.392]

ROSS, JOHN, b orn 1733 son of James Ross in Mill of Hole, minister of Kildonan, Sutherland, from 1761 to 1775, died 28 March 1775, husband of Ann Rose, parents of David and Katherine. [F.7.90]

ROSS, JOHN, a pewterer in Tain, Easter Ross, 1766. [OR#408]

ROSS, JOHN, a cooper in Tain, Easter Ross, 1766. [OR#408]

ROSS, JOHN, master of the Helen and Margaret of Cromarty, 1744. [NAS.E504.17.1]

ROSS, JOHN, in Octew, a soldier in Captain Hugh McLeod of Geanies Independent Company on 17 June 1746. [TGSI.LIII.381]

ROSS, JOHN, in Inverchasley, a soldier of the Master of Ross' Independent Company at Linachan, 14 June 1746. [TGSI.LIII.391]

ROSS, JOHN, in Glencalvy, a soldier of the Master of Ross' Independent Company at Linachan, 14 June 1746. [TGSI.LIII.392]

ROSS, JOHN, in Luncoinich, a soldier of the Master of Ross' Independent Company at Linachan, 14 June 1746. [TGSI.LIII.392]

ROSS, JOHN, was served heir to his father Robert Ross of Achnacloich who died in February 1757, on 6 September 1759. [NAS.SH]

ROSS, JOHN, in Tain, Easter Ross, 1766. [OR#409]

ROSS, JOHN, a silversmith in Tain, Easter Ross, 1766. [OR#408]

ROSS, JOHN, in Brachadir, Tain, Easter Ross, 1766. [OR#409]

ROSS, LACHLAN, soldier of Captain George Mackay's Independent Company at Shiromore, 1746. [TGSI.LIII.371]

ROSS, LACHLAN, a mason in Tain, Easter Ross, 1766. [OR#408]

ROSS, LACHLAN, with his wife, and four children, in Drumbeg, Assynt, Sutherland, 1774. [SA#79]

ROSS, MALCOLM, in Tulemlare, a soldier of the Master of Ross' Independent Company at Linachan, 14 June 1746. [TGSI.LIII.391]

ROSS, MARY, widow of John McLeod, tenant in Dornie, 1770. [NAS.E746.167.4]

ROSS, MERAN, born 1759, died 29 July 1788 in Achigorn. [Balnakeil gravestone, Sutherland]

ROSS, MURDOCH, a merchant in Tain, Easter Ross, 1766. [OR#408]

ROSS, NICHOLAS, a merchant in Tain, Easter Ross, 1766. [OR#408]

ROSS, PAUL, in Octew, a soldier in Captain Hugh McLeod of Geanies Independent Company on 17 June 1746. [TGSI.LIII.381]

ROSS, ROBERT, in Ardoch, soldier of George Munro of Culcairns' Independent Company, 1745. [TGSI.LIII.365]

ROSS, ROBERT, in Lubreach, a soldier in Captain Hugh McLeod of Geanies Independent Company on 17 June 1746. [TGSI.LIII.381]

ROSS, ROBERT, formerly a soldier in a Highland Independent Company, then tacksman of Drimvaich, 1756. [NAS.E746.113.6/1]

ROSS, ROBERT, a corporal of the Master of Ross' Independent Company at Linachan, 14 June 1746. [TGSI.LIII.391]

ROSS, ROBERT, in Kindease, a soldier of the Master of Ross' Independent Company at Linachan, 14 June 1746. [TGSI.LIII.391]

ROSS, RODERICK, a merchant in Tain, Easter Ross, 1766. [OR#408]

ROSS, THOMAS, in Knokan, a soldier in Captain Hugh McLeod of Geanies Independent Company on 17 June 1746. [TGSI.LIII.380]

ROSS, THOMAS, in Tain, Easter Ross, a soldier of the Master of Ross' Independent Company at Linachan, 14 June 1746. [TGSI.LIII.392]

ROSS, THOMAS, was served heir to his father Thomas Ross of Calrossie, Ross-shire, who died in April 1755, on 27 October 1758. [NAS.SH]

ROSS, THOMAS, tenant in Eastside of Mey, Caithness, 1771. [NAS.GD96.679.14]

ROSS, THOMAS, minister in Tain, Easter Ross, 1766. [OR#409]

ROSS, WALTER, born 1678 son of Alexander Ross of Torranlish, educated at Marischal College, Aberdeen, minister of Kilmuir Easter, Ross and Cromarty, from 1715 to 1733, died 29 December 1733. Husband of Catherine Wilson. [F.7.58]

ROSS, WALTER, minister of Tongue, Sutherland, from 1730 to 1761, died 9 September 1762. Husband of Annabella Stewart and father of Barbara. [F.7.110]

ROSS, WALTER, in Aldanguich, a soldier of the Master of Ross' Independent Company at Linachan, 14 June 1746. [TGSI.LIII.392]

ROSS, WALTER, in Tain, Easter Ross, a soldier of the Master of Ross' Independent Company at Linachan, 14 June 1746. [TGSI.LIII.392]

ROSS, WALTER, graduated MA from Marischal College in 1771, minister of Clyne parish, Sutherland, from 1777 to 1825. He married Elizabeth, daughter of Captain John Sutherland tenant of Clyneleish, on 16 February 1787, parents of William Baillie born 1790, and Janet born and died 1793. [F.7.80]

ROSS, WILLIAM, in Clynes, soldier of George Munro of Culcairns' Independent Company, 1745. [TGSI.LIII.365]

ROSS, WILLIAM, in Gainies, a soldier in Captain Hugh McLeod of Geanies Independent Company on 17 June 1746. [TGSI.LIII.380]

ROSS, WILLIAM, in Drumnvaich, a soldier of the Master of Ross' Independent Company at Linachan, 14 June 1746. [TGSI.LIII.392]

ROSS, WILLIAM, in Rarrichies, a soldier of the Master of Ross' Independent Company at Linachan, 14 June 1746. [TGSI.LIII.392]

ROSS, WILLIAM, in Lubcroy, a soldier of the Master of Ross' Independent Company at Linachan, 14 June 1746. [TGSI.LIII.392]

ROSS, WILLIAM, in Aldannasackaile, a soldier of the Master of Ross' Independent Company at Linachan, 14 June 1746. [TGSI.LIII.392]

ROSS, WILLIAM, in Crech, soldier of Captain George Mackay's Independent Company at Shiromore, 1746. [TGSI.LIII.371]

ROSS, WILLIAM, the elder, soldier of Captain George Mackay's Independent Company at Shiromore, 1746. [TGSI.LIII.371]

ROSS, WILLIAM, the younger, soldier of Captain George Mackay's Independent Company at Shiromore, 1746. [TGSI.LIII.371]

ROSS, WILLIAM, in Badarichin, a soldier of the Master of Ross' Independent Company at Linachan, 14 June 1746. [TGSI.LIII.391]

ROSS, WILLIAM, in Tulimtarvie, a soldier of the Master of Ross' Independent Company at Linachan, 14 June 1746. [TGSI.LIII.392]

ROSS, WILLIAM, of Otterach, a merchant in Tain, Easter Ross, 1766. [OR#408]

ROSS, WILLIAM, a soldier in Tain, Easter Ross, 1766. [OR#409]

ROSS, WILLIAM, a wright in Tain, Easter Ross, 1766. [OR#408]

ROY, ALEXANDER, in Tain, Easter Ross, 1766. [OR#409]

ROY, or MCLEOD, ALEXANDER, with his wife, and three children, in Culaig, Assynt, Sutherland, 1774. [SA#77]

ROY, or MCLEOD, ANGUS, with his wife, four children, and one servant, in Inverkirkaig, Assynt, Sutherland, 1774. [SA#81]

ROY, DAVID, in Tain, Easter Ross, 1766. [OR#409]

ROY, FRANCIS, in Tain, Easter Ross, 1766. [OR#409]

ROY, JOHN MACLEOD, with his wife, and two children, in Leadbeg, Assynt, Sutherland, 1774. [SA#83]

ROY, or MCKENZIE, KENNETH, with his wife, and two children, in Clashmore, Assynt, Sutherland, 1774. [SA#75]

ROY, MURDOCH, in Knockintied, soldier of Captain Colin Mackenzie's Independent Company, 1746. [TGSI.LIII.385]

ROY, RORY, in Tronimbrass, Applecross, Wester Ross, 1718. [TGSI.LIV.450]

RUGG, WILLIAM, a cottar in Gills, Mey, Caithness, 1771. [NAS.GD96.679.14]

SAGE, ANN, born 1762, died 22 April 1770. [Lochcarron. Wester Ross, gravestone]

SAGE, EANEAS, born 1694, late minister at Lochcarron, died 15 July 1774. [Lochcarron, Wester Ross, gravestone]

SAGE, JOHN, schoolmaster and catechist at Ullapool, Sutherland, 1759. [NAS.E746.84/131]

SAGE, LILLA, born 1760, died in May 1770. [Lochcarron, Wester Ross, gravestone]

SCOBIE, JAMES, born 25 September 1735, son of William Scobie in Assynt. Minister of Wick, Caithness, from 1762 to 1764, died 3 July 1764. Husband of Elizabeth Calder. [F.7.142]

SCOBIE, JOHN, tenant farmer, Cromalt, Assynt, Sutherland, 1775. [SA#67]

SCOBIE, JOHN, in Cromauld, Assynt, Sutherland, 1774. [SA#77]

SCOBIE, KENNETH, and his son John, tenant farmer in Achmore, and Little Assynt, Sutherland, 1766, and in 1775; with his wife, seven children and six servants, in Auchmore, and in Rhintraid, Assynt, Sutherland, 1774. [SA#66/71/84/86]

SCOBIE, WILLIAM, licensed by the Presbytery of Strathbogie in 1727 and appointed missionary to the parish; called by the Presbytery of Dornoch and ordained 12 September 1728 as minister of the parish of Assynt,

Sutherland, died 24 November 1763. He married Jane, daughter of John Mackay of Kirtomy on 3 March 1731. She died 19 February 1762. They had several children, Kenneth born 1732, John born 1733, James born 1735, Elizabeth born 1738, Janet born 1740, William born 1744, died 1745, Katherine born and died 1745, and George born 1747, died 1748. [F.7.78][NAS.E741.20.21]

SHAND, JOHN, a miller in Tain, Easter Ross, 1766. [OR#409]

SHILTHOMAS, WILLIAM, tailor in Thurso, Caithness, eldest son of the late James Shilthomas a glover there, 1739. [NAS.GD139.117]

SIMPSON, ALEXANDER, a corporal of the Master of Ross' Independent Company at Linachan, died in 1746. [TGSI.LIII.391]

SIMPSON, ALEXANDER, a smith, a soldier of the Master of Ross' Independent Company at Linachan, 14 June 1746. [TGSI.LIII.392]

SIMPSON, ALEXANDER, in Corninly, a soldier of the Master of Ross' Independent Company at Linachan, 14 June 1746. [TGSI.LIII.392]

SIMPSON, DONALD, in Langwell, a soldier of the Master of Ross' Independent Company at Linachan, 14 June 1746. [TGSI.LIII.392]

SIMPSON, HUGH, in Tain, Easter Ross, a soldier of the Master of Ross' Independent Company at Linachan, 14 June 1746. [TGSI.LIII.391]

SIMPSON, HUGH, in Garlomy, a soldier of the Master of Ross' Independent Company at Linachan, 14 June 1746. [TGSI.LIII.392]

SIMPSON, JAMES, a cottar in Mey, Caithness, 1771. [NAS.GD96.679.14]

SIMPSON, JOHN, a tidewaiter in Wick, Caithness, 1753.
[NAS.B73.2/1/12-13]

SIMPSON, MATTHEW, tenant in Mey, Caithness, 1771.
[NAS.GD96.679.14]

SIMPSON, THOMAS, born 1718, minister of Avoch, Presbytery of Chanonry, 1756 to 1786, died 22 September 1786. Husband of (1) Isobel, daughter of George McKenzie of Pitlundie and Culbo, parents of William (1757-1799); (2) Isobel, daughter of George Mackenzie of Gruinard and Elizabeth Forbes, parents of George, John, Alexander, Jean, Thomas, Margaret, Roderick, Duncan, and Geddes. [F.7.2]

SIMPSON, WILLIAM, tenant in Eastside of Mey, Caithness, 1771. [NAS.GD96.679.14]

SIMSON, GEORGE, a merchant in Tain, Easter Ross, 1766.
[OR#408]

SIMSON, HUGH, a silversmith in Tain, Easter Ross, 1766.
[OR#408]

SIMSON, WILLIAM, in Teanaird, soldier of George Munro of Culcairns' Independent Company, 1745.
[TGSI.LIII.365]

SINCLAIR, ALEXANDER, of Barrock, 1768.
[NAS.SC14.78.18]

SINCLAIR, ANN, with his two children, in Clasnhessie, Assynt, Sutherland, 1774. [SA#76]

SINCLAIR, CHARLES, of Stirkoke, 1772.
[NAS.SC14.78.19]

SINCLAIR, DONALD, soldier of Captain Hugh McKay's Independent Company, 17 June 1746. [TGSI.LIII.390]

SINCLAIR, DONALD, a cottar in Mey, Caithness, 1771.
[NAS.GD96.679.14]

SINCLAIR, DUNCAN, with his wife, and one child, in Culin, Kirkton, Assynt, Sutherland, 1774. [SA#82]

SINCLAIR, ESTHER, spouse of Reverend John Sinclair of Forss, Caithness, minister at Watten, Caithness, and daughter of the late Alexander Sinclair of Olrig, Caithness, 1743. [NAS.GD139.74]

SINCLAIR, GEORGE, of Ulbster, provost of Wick, Caithness, 1739. [NAS.B73.2/1/8]

SINCLAIR, GEORGE, in Dalhalva, soldier of Captain Hugh McKay's Independent Company, 17 June 1746. [TGSI.LIII.390]

SINCLAIR, GEORGE, of Ulbster, Caithness, 1747. [NAS.SC14.78.17/10]

SINCLAIR, GEORGE, a tenant in Delalvah, Halladale, Caithness, 1756. [NAS.GD87.SEC2.13]

SINCLAIR, GEORGE, of Geise, son and heir of the late Robert Sinclair of Geise, advocate, 1761. [NAS.GD139.119; GD87.Sec.2/9, 11]

SINCLAIR, GEORGE, in Ulbster, Caithness, 1770. [NAS.RD2.208.676/681/783]

SINCLAIR, GEORGE, a cottar in Mey, Caithness, 1771. [NAS.GD96.679.14]

SINCLAIR, HUGH, in Achervordevin, soldier of Captain Hugh McKay's Independent Company, 17 June 1746. [TGSI.LIII.391]

SINCLAIR, Sir JAMES, of Mey, Caithness, testament, 1736. [NAS.GD96.683.1]

SINCLAIR, JAMES, of Holburnhead, around 1760. [NAS.GD87.Sec.2/16]

SINCLAIR, JAMES, a cottar in Mey, Caithness, 1771. [NAS.GD96.679.14]

SINCLAIR, JANET, a widow, in Culaig, Assynt, Sutherland, 1774. [SA#77]

SINCLAIR, JOHN, of Brims, Caithness, 1725. [NAS.SC14.78.17/6]

SINCLAIR, JOHN, of Ulbster, Caithness, 1732. [NAS.SC14.78.17/7]

SINCLAIR, JOHN, born 1706, son of John Sinclair of Forse, Caithness, and Barbara Sinclair. Minister of Watten, Caithness, from 1733 to 1753, died 1 May 1753. Husband of Esther Sinclair, and father of Alexander. [F.7.139]

SINCLAIR, JOHN, of Forss, Caithness, brother of James Sinclair and of Dr William Sinclair, letters 1739-1769. [NAS.GD87.Sec.2/9]

SINCLAIR, JOHN, a tenant in Earr, Halladale, Caithness, 1756. [NAS.GD87.SEC2.13]

SINCLAIR, JOHN, in Sibsterwick, Caithness, 1770. [NAS.RD4.207.240]

SINCLAIR, JOHN, tenant in Eastside of Mey, Caithness, 1771. [NAS.GD96.679.14]

SINCLAIR, Sir JOHN, of Mey, Caithness, testament, 1774. [NAS.GD96.683.1]

SINCLAIR, KENNETH, a grasskeeper, in Fillin, Assynt, Sutherland, 1774. [SA#80]

SINCLAIR, ROBERT, of Giese, 1732-1744. [NAS.GD87.Sec.2/6]

SINCLAIR, WILLIAM, in Stemster, Caithness, 1730s. [NAS.SC14.78.30]

SINCLAIR, WILLIAM, of Freswick, Caithness, 1725. [NAS.GD139.203]

SINCLAIR, WILLIAM, a physician in Thurso, Caithness, 1758. [NAS.GD87.Sec.2/15]

SINCLAIR, WILLIAM, tenant in Mey, Caithness, 1771. [NAS.GD96.679.14]

SINCLAIR, WILLIAM, tenant in Mill of Mey, Caithness, 1771. [NAS.GD96.679.14]

SINCLAIR, WILLIAM, with his wife and three children, in Badinamban, Assynt, Sutherland, 1774. [SA#74]

SKELDOCH, JOHN, minister of Kilmonivaig, Inverness, 1725 to 1734, then of Farr, Sutherland, from 1734 to 1753, died 25 June 1753. Husband of Jane Thrift. [F.7.107]

SKINNER, JOHN, a weaver in Tain, Easter Ross, 1766. [OR#409]

SLEASON, JAMES, sailor or fisherman settled at New Tarbat, Easter Ross, 1765. [NAS.E746.80]

SMART, JOHN, a tailor in Tain, Easter Ross, 1766. [OR#408]

SMITH, ALEXANDER, born 1737. Minister of Olrig, Caithness, from 1762 to 1784, died 19 December 1784. Husband of Elizabeth Sinclair, and father of William, John, Jean, Thomas, James, Margaret, and Alexander. [F.7.129]

SMITH, JAMES, born 1684, minister of Creich, Sutherland, from 1731 to 1758, husband of Katherine Munro, and father of Christian, Katherine, George, John, Elizabeth and Isobel, died on 17 November 1758. [F.7.82]

SMITH, JOHN, in Toskaig, Applecross, Wester Ross, 1718. [TGSI.LIV.452]

SMITH, MALCOLM, in Toskaig, Applecross, Wester Ross, 1718. [TGSI.LIV.452]

STEUART, GEORGE, in Nonokeil, a soldier in Captain Hugh McLeod of Geanies Independent Company on 17 June 1746. [TGSI.LIII.380]

STEWART, ALEXANDER, with his wife, and two children, in Glenlerag, Assynt, Sutherland, 1774. [SA#80]

STEWART, DONALD, tacksman of Dingwall, Ross and Cromarty, 1766-1773. [NAS.GD46.SEC.1/212]

STEWART, GEORGE, tacksman of Urray, Ross and Cromarty, 1767-1773, [NAS.GD46.SEC.1/212]

STEWART, JOHN, in Bolnain, soldier of Captain Colin Mackenzie's Independent Company, 1746. [TGSI.LIII.385]

STEWART, JOHN, in Nedd, Assynt, Sutherland, 1774. [SA#85]

STEWART, NEILL, in Thurso, Caithness, 1743. [NAS.GD84/2/27]

STEWART, THOMAS, tacksman of Urray, Ross and Cromarty, 1767. [NAS.GD46.SEC.1/212]

STEWART, WILLIAM, tacksman of Urray, Ross and Cromarty, 1767-1773. [NAS.GD46.SEC.1/212]

STRONACH, ALEXANDER, schoolmaster in the barony of Coigach, 1765-1771. [NAS.E746.84]

SUTHERLAND, ADAM, in Achintell, soldier of Alexander Gunn's Independent Company at Shiromore, 16 June 1746. [TGSI.LIII.369]

SUTHERLAND, ALEXANDER, in Ardoch, soldier of George Munro of Culcairns' Independent Company, 1745. [TGSI.LIII.365]

SUTHERLAND, ALEXANDER, in Lurible, soldier of Alexander Gunn's Independent Company at Shiromore, 16 June 1746. [TGSI.LIII.369]

SUTHERLAND, ALEXANDER, a merchant in Thurso, Caithness, 4 July 1751. [NAS.RD4.177/1.285]

SUTHERLAND, ALEXANDER, a soldier of Captain Hugh McKay's Independent Company in 1746. [TGSI.LIII.391]

SUTHERLAND, ALEXANDER, born 1704, a gardener at Dunrobin, Sutherland, for 60 years, died in October 1784. [Golspie gravestone, Sutherland]

SUTHERLAND, ANDREW, born 1690 son of John Sutherland a tailor burgess of Dornoch, Sutherland. Schoolmaster at Wick the minister of Latheron and Dunbeath, Caithness, from 1717 to 1732, died in January 1732. Husband of Beatrix Mackay and father of John, James, George, Robert, William and Elizabeth. [F.7.125]

SUTHERLAND, ANDREW, soldier of Alexander Gunn's Independent Company at Shiromore, 16 June 1746. [TGSI.LIII.369]

SUTHERLAND, ANDREW, a tenant in Earr, Halladale, Caithness, 1756. [NAS.GD87.SEC2.13]

SUTHERLAND, DONALD, in Brora, Sutherland, soldier of Alexander Gunn's Independent Company at Shiromore, 16 June 1746. [TGSI.LIII.369]

SUTHERLAND, DONALD, in Achnichon, soldier of Alexander Gunn's Independent Company at Shiromore, 16 June 1746. [TGSI.LIII.369]

SUTHERLAND, DONALD, in Borible, soldier of Alexander Gunn's Independent Company at Shiromore, 16 June 1746. [TGSI.LIII.369]

SUTHERLAND, DONALD, a merchant in Thurso, Caithness, 1758. [NAS.GD84/2/47-48]

SUTHERLAND, DONALD, a weaver in Tain, Easter Ross, 1766. [OR#409]

SUTHERLAND, HUGH, minister at Kildonan, Sutherland, from 1740 to 1753; minister of Rogart, Sutherland, from 1753 to 1773, died 8 April 1773, husband of Janet McLean, parents of William and Alexander. [F.7.90/98]

SUTHERLAND, JAMES, of Langwell, Caithness, protest dated 25 January 1751, [NAS.RD2.169.103]

SUTHERLAND, Lieutenant Colonel JAMES, born 1726, died on 23 May 1789. [Golspie gravestone, Sutherland]

SUTHERLAND, JOHN, of Forss, Caithness, Captain of the Earl of Loudoun's Regiment at Dornoch, Sutherland, 10 March 1746. [MCP.V.30]

SUTHERLAND, JOHN, born in Dornoch, Sutherland, during 1731 son of William Sutherland, educated at St Andrews and graduated MA in 1759, minister at Dornoch from 1759 to 1777, died on 10 September 1777, husband of Elizabeth Sutherland, parents of several children including John born 1778 who died in Jamaica in 1806. [F.7.84]

SUTHERLAND, JOHN, son of Andrew Sutherland. Minister of Halkirk, Caithness, from 1745 to 1753, then went abroad. Husband of (1) Mary Preston, (2) Elizabeth mackay, and father of William, Hugh, and Solomon. [F.7.122]

SUTHERLAND, JOHN, in Keindonald, soldier of Alexander Gunn's Independent Company at Shiromore, 16 June 1746. [TGSI.LIII.369]

SUTHERLAND, JOHN, in Skinnet, soldier of Captain Hugh McKay's Independent Company, 17 June 1746. [TGSI.LIII.391]

SUTHERLAND, JOHN, a merchant in Golspie, Sutherland, 11 May 1751. [NAS.RD3.211/1.207]

SUTHERLAND, JOHN, son of Reverend Arthur Sutherland of Edderton, minister of Tain, Easter Ross, and Morinnis from 1752 to 1769, died 25 November 1769. Husband of (1) Christina Ross, parents of Elizabeth, Margaret, William, David, John, and Walter; (2) Ann Ross, parents of Sybilla, Donald, Janet, George, Simon, and Anne. [F.7.72]

SUTHERLAND, KENNETH, Ensign of the Sutherland Independent Company at Inverness 1745. [MCP.V.92]

SUTHERLAND, KENNETH, soldier of Captain George Mackay's Independent Company at Shiromore, 1746. [TGSI.LIII.371]

SUTHERLAND, MARION, daughter of the late Robert Sutherland, sometime tacksman in Ausdale, widow of Patrick Kennedy carpenter in Dunbeath, Caithness, and now spouse of Thomas Calder tenant in Banks of Scouthel, mother of Robert Kennedy, 1774. [NAS.GD139.239]

SUTHERLAND, NICOL, in Dornoch, Sutherland, soldier of Alexander Gunn's Independent Company at Shiromore, 16 June 1746. [TGSI.LIII.368]

SUTHERLAND, PETER or PATRICK, Captain of an Independent Company commanded by the Earl of Loudoun at Dornoch, 10 March 1746. [MCP.V.31/92]

SUTHERLAND, ROBERT, in Balcherry, soldier of George Munro of Culcairns' Independent Company, 1745. [TGSI.LIII.365]

SUTHERLAND, ROBERT, in Badloch, corporal of Alexander Gunn's Independent Company at Shiromore, 16 June 1746. [TGSI.LIII.368]

SUTHERLAND, ROBERT, the younger of Langwell, 1767. [NAS.GD139.231]

SUTHERLAND, WILLIAM, born 27 January 1738, son of John Sutherland in Tain, Easter Ross. Minister of Wick, Caithness, from 1765 to 1813, died 23 June 1816. Husband of Catherine Anderson, and father of William,

John, George, James, Elizabeth, Christian, David, Richard, Ramsay, Jane, Alexander, George, Catherine, Benjamin, Johanna, Alexandrina, Mary, James, and Margaret. [F.7.142]

SUTHERLAND, WILLIAM, in Thinerceena, soldier of Alexander Gunn's Independent Company at Shiromore, 16 June 1746. [TGSI.LIII.368]

SUTHERLAND, WILLIAM, of Wester, 1745. [NAS.GD139.40]

SUTHERLAND, WILLIAM, in Tain, Easter Ross, 1766. [OR#409]

SUTHERLAND, Mrs, in Castlehill, 1780. [NAS.E746.81]

SWANSON, DAVID, a shoemaker in Thurso, Caithness, 1758. [NAS.GD84/2/44]

SWANSON, ELSPET, tenant in Harrow, Mey, Caithness, 1771. [NAS.GD96.679.14]

SWANSON, HELEN, tenant in Eastside of Mey, Caithness, 1771. [NAS.GD96.679.14]

TAYLOR, FARQUHAR ROY, soldier of Captain Alexander Mackenzie's Independent Company, 1746. [TGSI.LIII.382]

TAYLOR, FINLAY, a shoemaker in Tain, Easter Ross, 1766. [OR#409]

TAYLOR, HUGH, a wigmaker in Tain, Easter Ross, 1766. [OR#408]

TAYLOR, JAMES, minister of Watten, Caithness, from 1754 to 1778, died 10 August 1778. Husband of Emilia Clark. [F.7.139]

TAYLOR, JOHN, a tailor in Tain, Easter Ross, 1766. [OR#408]

TAYLOR, WILLIAM, a weaver in Tain, Easter Ross, 1766. [OR#409]

TAYLOR, WILLIAM, sailor or fisherman settled at New Tarbat, Easter Ross, 1765. [NAS.E746.80]

THOMAS, WILLIAM MACCOLVIE, in Brahan, soldier of Captain Colin Mackenzie's Independent Company, 1746. [TGSI.LIII.385]

THOMPSON, WILLIAM, skipper in Dunbeath, Caithness, 1766. [NAS.GD139.231]

THOMSON, DONALD, in Culcairn, soldier of George Munro of Culcairns' Independent Company, 1745. [TGSI.LIII.365]

THOMSON, JOHN, born 1735 in Avoch, the Black Isle, schoolmaster at Golspie, minister of Durness, Sutherland, from 1764 to 1811, died 12 June 1811, husband of (1) Mary Robertson, (2) Margaret Clunes, (3) Christian Mackenzie, father of twelve children including Kenneth born 1766, died in Jamaica 1794, and Mackay, born 1784, died in Jamaica, 1803. [F.7.102]

TRAILL, GEORGE, of Hobbister, born 1723 son of George Traill and Isobel Louttit. Minister of Dunnet, Caithness, from 1751 to 1783, died 9 April 1785. Husband of Jean Murray, and father of Margaret, George, James, Isobel, and Barbara. [F.7.120]

URQUHART, DANIEL, master of the Betty of Cromarty, 1742. [NAS.E504.17.1]

URQUHART, DONALD, master of the Helen and Margaret of Cromarty, 1743. [NAS.E504.17.1]

URQUHART, DONALD, in Culbin, soldier of George Munro of Culcairns' Independent Company, 1745. [TGSI.LIII.365]

URQUHART, DONALD, in Kildinn, soldier of Captain, Colin Mackenzie's Independent Company, 1746. [TGSI.LIII.385]

URQUHART, GEORGE, in Alness, Easter Ross, soldier of George Munro of Culcairns' Independent Company, 1745. [TGSI.LIII.365]

URQUHART, GEORGE, a soldier in Captain Hugh McLeod of Geanies Independent Company on 17 June 1746. [TGSI.LIII.381]

URQUHART, JAMES, with his mother, in Unapool, Assynt, Sutherland, 1774. [SA#88]

URQUHART, JOHN, in Clunell, soldier of George Munro of Culcairns' Independent Company, 1745. [TGSI.LIII.365]

URQUHART, KATHERINE, wife of John Sutherland a mason at Dunrine, Dunrobin, Sutherland, died on 4 March 1754. [Golspie gravestone, Sutherland]

URQUHART, ROBERT, in Tain, Easter Ross, 1766. [OR#409]

URQUHART, RORY, with his wife, two children, and one servant, in Glenlerag, Assynt, Sutherland, 1774. [SA#80]

URQUHART, WILLIAM, in Ardoch, soldier of George Munro of Culcairns' Independent Company, 1745. [TGSI.LIII.365]

URQUHART, WILLIAM, post in Tain, Easter Ross, 1766. [OR#409]

WALLACE, ALEXANDER, in Dalbreack, Sutherland, soldier of George Munro of Culcairns' Independent Company, 1745. [TGSI.LIII.365]

WATSON, ANNABEL, with two children, in Inverkirkaig, Assynt, Sutherland, 1774. [SA#82]

WATSON, DONALD, with his wife, two children, and one servant, in Inverkirkaig, Assynt, Sutherland, 1774. [SA#82]

WATSON, GEORGE, minister of Kiltearn and Lemlair from 1770 to 1775. [F.7.43]

WATSON, JOHN, with his wife and servant, in Badinamban, Assynt, Sutherland, 1774. [SA#74]

WATSON, NORMAND, in Inverkirkaig, Assynt, Sutherland, 1774. [SA#82]

WHITE, PATRICK, in Dingwall, Ross and Cromarty, 1782. [NAS.E746.79]

WILLIAMSON, ALEXANDER, in Ardoch, soldier of George Munro of Culcairns' Independent Company, 1745. [TGSI.LIII.365]

WILLIAMSON, ALEXANDER, a cottar in Mey, Caithness, 1771. [NAS.GD96.679.14]

WILLIAMSON, DONALD, a cottar in Mey, Caithness, 1771. [NAS.GD96.679.14]

WINCHESTER, ROBERT, baillie of Wick, Caithness, 1737. [NAS.GD136.47]

WOOD, DAVID, sailor or fisherman settled at New Tarbat, Easter Ross, 1765. [NAS.E746.80]

WOOD, JOHN, born 1701, minister of Rosemarkie, Ross and Cromarty, from 1734 to 1770, died 10 November 1775. Husband of (1) Anne Ogilvie; (2) Sophia Irvine, parents of Alexander, Anne, John, John, Mary, Sophia, Charles, William, James, George, Joseph (emigrated to Jamaica), and Andrew. [F.7.23]

WRIGHT, HUGH, tenant in Mey, Caithness, 1771. [NAS.GD96.679.14]

WRIGHT, JAMES, tenant in Harrow, Mey, Caithness, 1771. [NAS.GD96.679.14]

WRIGHT, JOHN, a cottar in Mey, Caithness, 1771. [NAS.GD96.679.14]

YOUNG, GEORGE, an apothecary in Thurso, Caithness, 1732. [NAS.GD87.Sec.2/6]

YOUNG, JOHN, tenant in Eastside of Mey, Caithness, 1771. [NAS.GD96.679.14]